A Note From Rick Renner

I am on a personal quest to see a "revival of the Bible" so people can establish their lives on a firm foundation that will stand strong and endure the test as end-time storm winds begin to intensify.

In order to experience a revival of the Bible in your personal life, it is important to take time each day to read, receive, and apply its truths to your life. James tells us that if we will continue in the perfect law of liberty — refusing to be forgetful hearers, but determined to be doers — we will be blessed in our ways. As you watch or listen to the programs in this series and work through this corresponding study guide, I trust you will search the Scriptures and allow the Holy Spirit to help you hear something new from God's Word that applies specifically to your life. I encourage you to be a doer of the Word He reveals to you. Whatever the cost, I assure you — it will be worth it.

Thy words were found, and I did eat them;
and thy word was unto me the joy and rejoicing of mine heart:
for I am called by thy name, O Lord God of hosts.
— Jeremiah 15:16

Your brother and friend in Jesus Christ,

Rick Renner

How To Flourish in Your Senior Years
Proof That God Wants To Use You Mightily as You Age and Mature

Copyright © 2025 by Rick Renner
1814 W. Tacoma St.
Broken Arrow, OK 74012-1406

Published by Rick Renner Ministries
www.renner.org

ISBN 13: 978-1-6675-1138-2

ISBN 13 eBook: 978-1-6675-1139-9

How To Use This Study Guide

This ten-lesson study guide corresponds to *"How To Flourish in Your Senior Years" With Rick Renner* (Renner TV). Each lesson in this study guide covers a topic that is addressed during the program series, with questions and references supplied to draw you deeper into your own private study of the Scriptures on this subject.

To derive the most benefit from this study guide, consider the following:

First, watch or listen to the program prior to working through the corresponding lesson in this guide. (Programs can also be viewed at **renner.org** by clicking on the Media/Archives links or on our Renner Ministries YouTube channel.)

Second, take the time to look up the scriptures included in each lesson. Prayerfully consider their application to your own life.

Third, use a journal or notebook to make note of your answers to each lesson's Study Questions and Practical Application challenges.

Fourth, invest specific time in prayer and in the Word of God to consult with the Holy Spirit. Write down the scriptures or insights He reveals to you.

Finally, take action! Whatever the Lord tells you to do according to His Word, do it.

For added insights on this subject, it is recommended that you obtain Rick Renner's books *A Life Ablaze* and *Fallen Angels, Giants, Monsters, and the World Before the Flood.* You may also select from Rick's other available resources by placing your order at **renner.org** or by calling 1-800-742-5593.

TOPIC
God's Promise of Longevity

SCRIPTURES

1. **Genesis 6:3** — And the Lord said, My spirit shall not always strive with man, for that he also is flesh: yet his days shall be an hundred and twenty years.

2. **Psalm 90:10** — The days of our years are threescore years and ten; and if by reason of strength they be fourscore years, yet is their strength labour and sorrow; for it is soon cut off, and we fly away.

3. **Psalm 91:16** — With long life will I satisfy him, and shew him my salvation.

4. **Deuteronomy 4:40** — Thou shalt keep therefore his statutes, and his commandments, which I command thee this day, that it may go well with thee, and with thy children after thee, and that thou mayest prolong thy days upon the earth, which the Lord thy God giveth thee, for ever.

5. **Deuteronomy 5:33** — Ye shall walk in all the ways which the Lord your God hath commanded you, that ye may live, and that it may be well with you, and that ye may prolong your days in the land which ye shall possess.

6. **Deuteronomy 6:1,2** — Now these are the commandments, the statutes, and the judgments, which the Lord your God commanded to teach you, that ye might do them in the land whither ye go to possess it: that thou mightest fear the Lord thy God, to keep all his statutes and his commandments, which I command thee, thou, and thy son, and thy son's son, all the days of thy life; and that thy days may be prolonged.

7. **Deuteronomy 30:19,20** — I call heaven and earth to record this day against you, that I have set before you life and death, blessing and cursing: therefore choose life, that both thou and thy seed may live: that thou mayest love the Lord thy God, and that thou mayest obey his voice, and that thou mayest cleave unto him: for he is thy life, and the length of thy days....

8. **Exodus 20:12** — Honour thy father and thy mother: that thy days may be long upon the land which the Lord thy God giveth thee.

9. **1 Kings 3:14** — And if thou wilt walk in my ways, to keep my statutes and my commandments, as thy father David did walk, then I will lengthen thy days.

10. **Proverbs 3:1,2** — My son, forget not my law; but let thine heart keep my commandments: for length of days, and long life, and peace, shall they add to thee.

11. **Proverbs 4:10** — Hear, O my son, and receive my sayings; and the years of thy life shall be many.

12. **Proverbs 9:11**— For by me thy days shall be multiplied, and the years of thy life shall be increased.

13. **Proverbs 10:27** — The fear of the Lord prolongeth days: but the years of the wicked shall be shortened.

14. **Job 5:26** — Thou shalt come to thy grave in a full age, like as a shock of corn cometh in in his season.

15. **Genesis 25:7,8** — And these are the days of the years of Abraham's life which he lived, an hundred threescore and fifteen years. Then Abraham gave up the ghost, and died in a good old age, an old man, and full of years; and was gathered to his people.

16. **Deuteronomy 34:7** — And Moses was an hundred and twenty years old when he died: his eye was not dim, nor his natural force abated.

17. **Job 42:16,17** — After this lived Job an hundred and forty years, and saw his sons, and his sons' sons, even four generations. So Job died, being old and full of days.

18. **Psalm 103:5** — [God] Who satisfieth thy mouth with good things; so that thy youth is renewed like the eagle's.

19. **Isaiah 40:29-31** — He giveth power to the faint; and to them that have no might he increaseth strength. Even the youths shall faint and be weary, and the young men shall utterly fall: But they that wait upon the Lord shall renew their strength; they shall mount up with wings as eagles; they shall run, and not be weary; and they shall walk, and not faint.

SYNOPSIS

The ten lessons in this study titled *How To Flourish in Your Senior Years* will focus on the following topics:

- God's Promise of Longevity
- Enoch — Taken by God at 365 Years of Age
- Noah — Getting Started at 500 Years of Age
- Abraham — A Late Start at 75 Years of Age
- Sarah — A Mother at 90 Years of Age
- Moses — Launching Out at 80 Years of Age
- Caleb — Asking for a New Assignment at 85 Years of Age
- Daniel — In His Prime at More Than 90 Years of Age
- Anna the Prophetess — Spiritually Vital in Old Age
- John the Apostle — New Revelation at More Than 90 Years of Age

If we were to pick a tree to represent those in their senior years, it would have to be the redwoods. Amazingly, these trees live an average of 600 years, and many live up to 2,000 years, each growing to a height of more than 350 feet with a diameter of 22 feet.[1] Theses extraordinary specimens are a symbol of the long life God desires to give His people. Indeed, our later years are meant to be our most productive years, so if you are getting older, fear not! You are now entering the greatest fruit-bearing season of your life.

The emphasis of this lesson:

Throughout the Scriptures, God promises long life to those who love Him and obey His Word. Although many have misinterpreted the Bible to say we are only promised 70 to 80 years, a believer who walks with God and takes good care of his body and soul can live 120 years or longer. His perfect will is that you live until you are satisfied.

Many People Are Living Longer

As a rule, middle age is considered to be between 40 to 45 to about 60 to 65. In most countries, 64 years of age has long been considered the benchmark for being a senior citizen. At the time of this writing, for those living in the United States, age 65 is what the government officially considers a senior citizen, and as of the 2020 census, there are now more than 50 million Americans — or about 17 percent of the population — who are 65 or older.

Interestingly, seniors aged 65 to 69 are more likely than teenagers to have a job. In fact, a full 32 percent of those past retirement age have jobs, which can be really beneficial. Often, people who retire begin to sit around not knowing what to do and lacking purpose. Many times, their health even deteriorates and declines so quickly that many to pass from this life soon after retirement. Thus, having a job provides purpose for living.

The average life expectancy in the United States for women is 80.2 years, and for men, it is 74.8 years. What may surprise you is that in the last three decades, the U.S. centenarian population, which is the number of people aged 100 or older, has nearly *tripled*. It is projected that by 2050, at least 400,000 Americans will be 100 years old or older. Presently, the world is home to an estimated 722,000 centenarians. By 2054, the world-wide centenarian population will reach nearly 4 million, and if we make it to 2100, this number is predicted to increase to more than 20 million.

In light of these facts, we might say that the day of the Redwoods has arrived!

Many Believers Have Misinterpreted What the Bible Says About Our Lifespan

There is an interesting verse in Genesis 6:3, which says, "And the Lord said, My spirit shall not always strive with man, for that he also is flesh: yet his days shall be an hundred and twenty years." Some interpret this as a promise that we can live up to 120 years, but there is no reason someone can't live 120 years or even longer if he or she does what is necessary to take care of his or her body and soul. Only God knows how long a person can live in this modern era.

The fact is there are many scriptures that promise long life if the right conditions are met. Regrettably, many raised in traditional churches grew up wrongly hearing that God only promised 70 or 80 years of life, and they base that thinking on Psalm 90:10, which says, "The days of our years are threescore years and ten; and if by reason of strength they be fourscore years, yet is their strength labour and sorrow; for it is soon cut off, and we fly away."

At face value, it does appear that this verse says a person's lifespan is between 70 (threescore and ten years) and 80 (fourscore years), but we must take into consideration to whom this passage was written. Psalm 90:10 was written to the children of Israel who rebelled against God in the wilderness and forfeited their privilege to enter the Promised Land. Rather than let this disgruntled generation wander in misery for decades on end, God limited their misery and essentially said, "This particular rebellious generation will live no more than 70 to 80 years because I do not want them to wander in misery for years on end."

Therefore, the 70-to-80-year limitation in this verse had to do with God's mercy, and it was not to be claimed by all God's people. When the next generation of Israelites who cooperated with and obeyed God entered the Promised Land, many of them lived much longer than the 70-to-80-year lifespan referred to in Psalm 90:10. This is an example of how vital it is to understand who God is speaking to and why He is saying what He is saying.

The Bible Promises Long life to Those Who Love and Obey the Lord

The Word of God is filled with promises of a long, vibrant life for those who walk with the Lord. Longevity is His blessing to the obedient and faithful. Consider this promise:

With long life will I satisfy him, and shew him my salvation.
— Psalm 91:16

There are several important words in this verse, including the word "long." It is from a Hebrew word that speaks of *length*, and it implies *longevity*. The word "life" denotes *days*, and as a phrase, "long life" depicts *long days* or *a very long life*.

Next, notice the word "satisfy," which means *to have enough, to have plenty of*, or *to be fully satisfied*. If you want a verse to claim longevity, Psalm 91:16 is your verse because it guarantees it to those who abide in the shadow of the Almighty (*see* Psalm 91:1). This is God's promise that we can live until we reach the point of satisfaction.

Psalm 91:16 wraps up with God saying He will show us His *salvation*. In addition to long life, we should also claim that God is going to show us His "salvation," which is translated from a Hebrew word that means *deliverance, healing, prosperity, wholeness*, and *everything that is packed in His salvation*. That is what God wants to show us all the way to the end of our life.

A List of God's Promises
Guaranteeing Longevity

The blessing of long life is promised throughout the Scriptures. To help you really grasp this truth in your heart, take some time to meditate on these promises and let the Holy Spirit renew your mind.

> **Thou shalt keep therefore his statutes, and his commandments, which I command thee this day, that it may go well with thee, and with thy children after thee, and that thou mayest prolong thy days upon the earth, which the Lord thy God giveth thee, for ever.**
>
> **— Deuteronomy 4:40**

This verse says that when you obey God's Word, life is going to be better, and your obedience is not just going to affect you — it's going to benefit your children and grandchildren as well. Living a right life will "prolong your days upon the earth."

The Bible also declares:

> **Ye shall walk in all the ways which the Lord your God hath commanded you, that ye may live, and that it may be well with you, and that ye may prolong your days in the land which ye shall possess.**
>
> **— Deuteronomy 5:33**

> **Now these are the commandments, the statutes, and the judgments, which the Lord your God commanded to teach you, that ye might do them in the land whither ye go to possess it: that thou mightest fear the Lord thy God, to keep all his statutes and his commandments, which I command thee, thou, and thy son, and thy son's son, all the days of thy life; and that thy days may be prolonged.**
>
> **— Deuteronomy 6:1,2**

Again, we see that when we walk in the ways of the Lord, things are better in our life, and our lifespan is extended. These promises are generational and made by God to all who have a healthy, reverential fear of Him.

Toward the end of Deuteronomy, God prompted Moses to write:

I call heaven and earth to record this day against you, that I have set before you life and death, blessing and cursing: therefore choose life, that both thou and thy seed may live: That thou mayest love the Lord thy God, and that thou mayest obey his voice, and that thou mayest cleave unto him: for he is thy life, and the length of thy days....

— Deuteronomy 30:19,20

In Exodus, we find a powerful promise connected with the fifth commandment:

Honour thy father and thy mother: that thy days may be long upon the land which the Lord thy God giveth thee.

— Exodus 20:12

For those who hear, receive, and obey the commandments of God's Word — walking in them and keeping them — God repeatedly promises a long and peaceful life:

And if thou wilt walk in my ways, to keep my statutes and my commandments, as thy father David did walk, then I will lengthen thy days.

— 1 Kings 3:14

My son, forget not my law; but let thine heart keep my commandments: for length of days, and long life, and peace, shall they add to thee.

— Proverbs 3:1,2

Hear, O my son, and receive my sayings; and the years of thy life shall be many.

— Proverbs 4:10

For by me thy days shall be multiplied, and the years of thy life shall be increased.

— Proverbs 9:11

Like Deuteronomy 6:1 and 2, the book of Proverbs also promises longevity to those who fear the Lord:

The fear of the Lord prolongeth days: but the years of the wicked shall be shortened.

— Proverbs 10:27

And in the fifth chapter of Job we read:

> **Thou shalt come to thy grave in a full age, like as a shock of corn cometh in in his season.**
>
> —Job 5:26

How You Think and Believe About Aging Will Affect How Long You Live

Rick shared how when he was young, he would look at certain relatives that were about 60 years old and think that they looked really old. One of the primary reasons they appeared so aged was because they were thinking and believing wrong. Like so many people today, they believed that God only promised us 70 years of life — maybe 80, if we're lucky. So, around the time they reached 60 years old, they began to think they were coming to the end of their life.

But as we can see from the myriad of scriptures we just listed, God repeatedly promises longevity to all those who love Him and obey His Word. You can live much longer than 70 or 80 years if you walk in fellowship with Him, keep His commandments, and take care of your body.

Medical science now declares that if certain conditions could be met to drastically slow down the aging of cells, it could be possible for the human body to live up to 1,000 years, which is just about how long people lived before the Flood.

What this tells us is that the way most people have been thinking about aging and "old age" needs to change. Proverbs 23:7 says that as a person thinks in his heart "so is he." So, if you think you're old, you're probably going to get old. But if you're older and you begin to think that you've got a long race to run, you're probably going to live much longer. The way you think is really going to affect what you experience.

Clearly, we need to renew our minds about longevity. God promises a long and satisfying life to the faithful and obedient, and He does not limit His blessings of long life to 70 or 80 years — or even to 120 years as some claim. Psalm 91:16 says God's perfect will is for you to live until you are satisfied.

Post-Flood Patriarchs
Who Lived Beyond 100 Years

Have you ever looked through the pages of the Old Testament to see how long people lived? Their ages at the time they departed this life may surprise you. Consider these well-known individuals who walked with God and did their best to obediently keep His commandments:

Abraham (*estimated* **c. 1967 — 1792 B.C.**)[2]

The Bible identifies Abraham as the "father of faith" and the progenitor of the Hebrew people. There are 14 chapters that document many of the details of his life (*see* Genesis 12-25). The book of Genesis says this about the end of Abraham's earthly journey:

> **And these are the days of the years of Abraham's life which he lived, an hundred threescore and fifteen years. Then Abraham gave up the ghost, and died in a good old age, an old man, and full of years; and was gathered to his people.**
> **— Genesis 25:7,8**

Keep in mind, one "score" is 20 years, so when the Bible says Abraham's life was 100 plus 3 score and 15 years, we can calculate that he lived to be 175 years old. Interestingly, it does not say he ended up as an old, weak man. Instead, it appears that he was physically strong to his last breath.

Moses (*estimated* **c. 1543 — 1423 B.C.**)[2]

Approximately five centuries after Abraham, a man named Moses came to prominence, and he also lived a long, full life. The Bible tells us:

> **And Moses was an hundred and twenty years old when he died: his eye was not dim, nor his natural force abated.**
> **— Deuteronomy 34:7**

What an amazing verse! Moses' eyesight was clear, and he possessed mental acuity — the faculties of his mind and body remained sharp and strong his entire life just like Abraham. Remarkably, he was still physically strong all the way to the end of his 120-year life.

Job (*estimated* **c. 2027 — 1827 B.C.**)[2]

More than likely, you have heard about Job. The book bearing his name is understood to be the oldest book of the Bible, and scholars actually place his life less than a century before Abraham. Although he did face a series of horrific hardships, the Scripture documents that he lived an additional 140 years after his time of suffering.

> **After this lived Job an hundred and forty years, and saw his sons, and his sons' sons, even four generations. So Job died, being old and full of days.**
>
> —Job 42:16,17

Can you imagine seeing your grandchildren, your great grandchildren, and your great-great grandchildren grow up? That is what Job was blessed with. His life was not cut short, and he did not die a sick, weak man. When his long life ended, he was happy, satisfied, and "full of days" just like Abraham.

Isaac and Jacob (*estimated* c. 1867 — 1687 B.C./c. 1807 — 1660 B.C.)[2]

According to Scripture, Abraham was the father of Isaac, and Isaac became the father of Jacob when he was 60 years old (*see* Genesis 21:2,3; 25:26). Genesis 35:28 and 29 (*NKJV*) says that altogether, "…The days of Isaac were one hundred and eighty years. So Isaac breathed his last and died, and was gathered to his people, being old and full of days. And his sons Esau and Jacob buried him."

Meanwhile, Jacob became the father of the 12 tribes of Israel, and after reconnecting with his son Joseph, he took his entire family down into Egypt where he lived out the remainder of his life. The Bible says, "And Jacob lived in the land of Egypt seventeen years. So the length of Jacob's life was one hundred and forty-seven years" (Genesis 47:28, *NKJV*).

Supernatural Age Renewal Is a Promise From God

For those who walk with God and obediently follow His Word, Psalm 103:5 says, "[He] satisfieth thy mouth with good things; so that thy youth is renewed like the eagle's." There is no medical procedure, no series of treatments, no healing cream or supplement that can compare with the divine regenerative power of the Spirit of Almighty God! His strength is unmatched, and He gives it to those who are His own. The prophet Isaiah declared:

He giveth power to the faint; and to them that have no might he increaseth strength. Even the youths shall faint and be weary, and the young men shall utterly fall: but they that wait upon the Lord shall renew their strength; they shall mount up with wings as eagles; they shall run, and not be weary; and they shall walk, and not faint.

— Isaiah 40:29-31

The fact is, we are surrounded by contemporary examples of people who are renewing their minds to the truth that they can live a long, full life and be highly productive all the way to the end. New studies show that...

- The most productive age is from 60 to 70 years of age.

- The second most productive stage is from 70 to 80 years of age.

- The third most productive stage is from 50 to 60 years of age.

Did you know that...

- The average age of Nobel Prize winners is late 60s to early 70s.

- The average age of presidents of prominent companies is 57 to 60 years.

- The average age of pastors of the 100 largest churches in the U.S. is 71 years.

- The average age of individuals who become Popes is 78 years.

Believe it or not, the best years of your life are between the ages of 60 and 80. At 60, you begin to reach your potential, and this continues into your 80s. If you are between 60 and 70, you are in the best mental level of your life, and if you are between 70 and 80, you are in the second-best mental level of your life.

The first 30 years...you *learn*. The second 30 years...you *do*. The third 30 years...you *impart* to others.

Friend, we need to get our minds renewed and in line with God's promise of longevity for those who love and obey Him. Even secular statistics prove that our best, most productive years are our latter years. So, if you are among those who are older — especially if you are 65 or older — it's not the time for you to move off the playing field and just surrender to old age. Rather, it's time to rethink your age and to embrace the most productive season of your life! You have more wisdom, more experience, and you are more fully primed and exercised mentally to be more successful than ever.

STUDY QUESTIONS

Study to shew thyself approved unto God, a workman that
needeth not to be ashamed, rightly dividing the word of truth.
— 2 Timothy 2:15

1. Were you aware of Psalm 90:10 and its declaration of a 70-to-80-year lifespan? If so, what did you understand it to mean previously? How do you see God's will for our lifespan differently after going through this lesson?

2. Do you have days where you are simply exhausted and drained by life? God has a supernatural prescription for you! Take these two spiritual supplements every day — put them in your mouth by declaring them out loud over your life and watch how God works!

Have you not known? Have you not heard? The everlasting
God, the Lord, the Creator of the ends of the earth, does not
faint or grow weary; there is no searching of His understanding.

He gives power to the faint and weary, and to him who has no
might He increases strength [causing it to multiply and making
it to abound].
— Isaiah 40:28,29 (*AMPC*)

I have strength for all things in Christ Who empowers me [I
am ready for anything and equal to anything through Him
Who infuses inner strength into me; I am self-sufficient in
Christ's sufficiency].
— Philippians 4:13 (*AMPC*)

PRACTICAL APPLICATION

But be ye doers of the word, and not hearers only,
deceiving your own selves.
— James 1:22

1. Of all the data regarding people living longer, the age and activity of retirees, and the growing centenarian population, which did you consider most enlightening? Why?

2. Did you know that many of the post-flood patriarchs lived well beyond the age of 100? How are your heart and mind stirred when you hear that Abraham lived to 175, Isaac lived to 180, Jacob lived to 147, Moses lived to 120, and Job lived well over 140 years?

---

[1] Redwood facts, National Park Service (https://www.nps.gov/redw/learn/nature /about-the-trees.htm; accessed 12/3/24).

[2] Estimated lifespan dates of the post-flood patriarchs adapted from *The Reese Chronological Bible* (Bloomington, MN: Bethany House Publishers, 1977).

LESSON 2

TOPIC
Enoch — Taken by God at 365 Years of Age

SCRIPTURES

1. **Psalm 91:16** — With long life will I satisfy him, and shew him my salvation.

2. **Mark 12:30** — And thou shalt love the Lord thy God with all thy heart, and with all thy soul, and with all thy mind, and with all thy strength....

3. **Genesis 5:18** — And Jared lived an hundred sixty and two years, and he begat Enoch.

4. **Genesis 5:21-24** — And Enoch lived sixty and five years, and begat Methuselah: and Enoch walked with God after he begat Methuselah three hundred years, and begat sons and daughters: and all the days of Enoch were three hundred sixty and five years: and Enoch walked with God: and he was not; for God took him

5. **Hebrews 11:5** — By faith Enoch was translated that he should not see death; and was not found, because God had translated him: for before his translation he had this testimony, that he pleased God.

6. **Jude 14,15** — And Enoch also, the seventh from Adam, prophesied of these, saying, Behold, the Lord cometh with ten thousands of his saints, to execute judgment upon all, and to convince all that are ungodly among them of all their ungodly deeds which they have ungodly committed, and of all their hard speeches which ungodly sinners have spoken against him.

GREEK WORDS

1. "translated" — **μετατίθημι** (*metatithimi*): to translate; to transfer

2. "not" — **οὐχ** (*ouch*): emphatically not

3. "found" — **εὑρίσκω** (*heurisko*): to find; to discover; a discovery made as a result of careful observation; a moment when one makes a surprising or conclusive discovery; points to a discovery made due to an intense investigation, scientific study, or scholarly research

4. "testimony" — **μαρτυρέω** (*martureo*): a testimony in a court of law; where we get the word martyr, which is one who suffers unjustly for what he believes; implies that Enoch likely suffered skepticism from those who heard him declare he would never die

SYNOPSIS

The age of the redwoods has arrived! Those who are devoted and obedient to the Lord Jesus Christ are like giant redwoods that keep growing bigger, reaching higher, and living longer. God is calling His people to embrace longevity so they will mature and live more meaningful, fruitful lives as they age.

We saw in our first lesson that the Bible is filled with promises guaranteeing long life for everyone who walks with the Lord and obeys His Word. Abraham, Isaac, and Jacob as well as Moses, Job, and many others all lived long lives and accomplished great things — especially in their senior years.

Your best, most productive days are not behind you — they are in front of you! It's time to renew your mind and bring it in line with God's promise of longevity. In this lesson, we will take a close look at the life of Enoch and see how he served the Lord up to the age of 365.

The emphasis of this lesson:

Enoch is revered as the first prophet of the Old Testament. He walked with God so closely that he was able to see more than 5,000 years into the future and describe the Second Coming of Christ. Enoch reached his peak of productivity at age 365 — that is when he had his greatest experience with God.

God Wants To Satisfy You
With a Very Long, Full Life

Psalm 91:16 is our anchor verse, and it says, "With long life will I satisfy him, and shew him my salvation." God wants to show you His salvation! The word "salvation" describes a package of blessings that includes *prosperity, wholeness, mental soundness, health*, and *healing*, which means God doesn't want you to get old and become feeble. He wants you to experience the fullness of His salvation all the way to the end of your life.

Looking at the beginning of this verse, we see that God wants to give you *long life*, and the word "long" is from a Hebrew term that speaks of *length of days* or *longevity*. Moreover, the word "life" in Hebrew is the word for *days*. As a phrase, "long life" depicts *long days* or *a very, very long life*. That is what God wants to satisfy you with. The word "satisfy" is from a word that means *to have enough, to have plenty of*, or *to be fully satisfied*.

Taking the meaning of all these words into consideration, we can see that Psalm 91:16 is God crying out to you through the pages of Scripture and saying, "Hey! Don't check out too early. I want to satisfy you with longevity. You don't have to leave this earth until you're fully satisfied with a very long life."

Our Lifespan Is Not Limited
to 70 or 80 Years

Now, as we saw in Lesson 1, many believers wrongly believe that God has only promised 70 or 80 years of life, and they base their belief on Psalm 90:10 (*NKJV*), which says, "The days of our lives are seventy years; and if by reason of strength they are eighty years...." This verse was written by Moses to the children of Israel who rebelled against God in the wilderness and forfeited their privilege to enter the Promised Land. Rather than let this disgruntled generation wander in misery for decades on end, God put a cap on the length of their life of no more than 70 to 80 years.

Thus, this limitation is an expression of God's mercy, and it was not to be claimed by all God's people. When the next generation of Israelites who cooperated with and obeyed God entered the Promised Land, many of them lived much longer than the 70-to-80-year lifespan referred to in Psalm 90:10.

Today, when those who believe our lifespan is limited to 70 to 80 years hit the age of 60, they begin to look old, feel old, and behave old all because they *think* old. The fact is, people today are living longer than previous generations because they are renewing their minds to the truth that it is God's will to satisfy His people with long, full lives.

New Studies Reveal
Our Best Years Are Our Senior Years

It is very encouraging to see that some of the latest scientific research shows that our latter years are actually our most productive years. Looking once again at these eye-opening facts we saw at the end of our last lesson, we learned that…

- The most productive age is from 60 to 70 years of age.
- The second most productive stage of life is from 70 to 80 years of age.
- The third most productive stage is from 50 to 60 years of age.

Of course, many people who are in their 50s and 60s are thinking about retirement, but if you're in that age bracket, that should be one of the last things on your mind because you are about to reach your peak somewhere between your 60s and 70s. In fact, when you're between 60 and 70, you're in the best mental stage of your life, and the second-best mental stage is between 70 and 80. Did you know that?

According to recent research…

- The average age of Nobel Prize winners is late 60s to early 70s.
- The average age of presidents of prominent companies is 57 to 60 years.
- The average age of pastors of the 100 largest churches in the U.S. is 71 years.

- The average age of individuals who become Popes is 78 years.

Just think — what if these Nobel Prize winners would have quit earlier in their life? They would have missed out on their greatest achievements. How about pastors? So many of them retire much earlier than 71, and they fail to benefit from the most productive time of their life.

If you think about it, the first 30 years of life are your time to *learn*. The second 30 years are your time to *work* and *do*. And the third set of 30 years is when you *help others* and *impart wisdom*.

Believe it or not, your best years are between 60 and 80 years of age. At 60, you begin to reach your potential, and this continues into your 80s. So, if you are 60 years old or older, you should embrace these findings by faith and begin to declare that your best years in life are still to come.

Don't Buy the Lie!
Age Is a PLUS, Not a Minus

It is a grave mistake and a lie of the enemy for older people to believe they're irrelevant due to their age. Age makes you better and gives you time to mature, grow, and gain priceless experience. When you're older, you finally have a greater understanding of how to walk with God, discern right from wrong, and have a much better handle on what you're called to do.

If you're hearing condemning thoughts telling you you're too old, irrelevant, or out of touch because of your age, that's the enemy speaking to you — don't listen to him. Nothing would make Satan happier than for you to believe the lies he's whispering. He'd love nothing more than to cause you to leave the playing field and sit on the sidelines just as you're coming into your most productive years. Friend, your senior years hold the greatest anointing, the greatest revelation, and the greatest productivity for your life.

We're told in Psalm 84:7 that it's God's plan for us to go from *strength to strength*, not from strength to weakness or from strength to sickness and being feeble. Thank God that in our time, many people are finally beginning to change the way they think about age. This is partly due to diet, partly to medical breakthroughs, and partly because people around us are living longer.

Today, we are surrounded by a cloud of contemporary witnesses who've run long races and who are still running strong and serving robustly into years way beyond what others have considered to be the norm. These trail blazers are setting a new standard for the rest of us. Because of their example, we are now seeing that with God's grace, it's possible to live a long life, run a strong race, and become more valuable and usable with age all the way to the end of our life.

So don't buy the lie that God only promised you only 70 or 80 years of life. If you believe that and aim for 70 or 80 years, that's probably what you'll get. However, if you aim at a longer life — like 90, 100, or 120 years — you'll come a lot closer to it. Jesus said, "…All things are possible to him that believeth" (Mark 9:23). Make sure you're believing for the right things. Stay spiritually vibrant, on track with God's Word, filled with His Spirit, and engaged in God-given relationships.

And by all means, take care of yourself and stay physically fit. Jesus said, "Thou shalt love the Lord thy God with all thy *heart*, and with all thy *soul*, and with all thy *mind*, and with all thy *strength*…" (Mark 12:30). You must take care of your whole being — spirit, soul, and body — if you're going to live a long life. Ask God to help you keep eating right, remaining active, and exercising so you can accomplish His will. All these factors are vital for your longevity.

The Life of Enoch

For our first example of longevity, we turn our attention to a man named *Enoch*. The Bible says, "And Jared lived an hundred sixty and two years, and he begat Enoch" (Genesis 5:18). Thus, Jared was the father of Enoch, and Enoch was the seventh generation from Adam. His name means *to teach* or *to correct*, and it was during his lifetime that the world was experiencing very dark and nefarious activities. It appears that Enoch was sent *to teach* or *to bring correction* to a generation that had really drifted away from God.

The Bible goes on to tell us, "…Enoch lived sixty and five years, and begat Methuselah" (Genesis 5:21). Interestingly, the name "Methuselah" means, *his death shall bring* or *when he dies, it will come*. Enoch understood the prophetic meaning of his son's name and the significance of his birth. When Methuselah died, the judgment of God would come upon the earth to purge it of all the widespread wickedness.

Methuselah was the oldest man to ever live and die, having a lifespan of 969 years (*see* Genesis 5:27). The longevity of his life demonstrates God's immense patience and mercy, not wishing that anyone should be judged and perish.

Enoch walked with God.

Of all the things the Bible could have recorded about Enoch's life, the attribute it notes twice is that he *walked with God.* Genesis 5:22-24 tells us:

> **And Enoch walked with God after he begat Methuselah three hundred years, and begat sons and daughters: and all the days of Enoch were three hundred sixty and five years: and Enoch walked with God: and he was not; for God took him.**

If you remember, in Lesson 1, we saw that the Bible repeatedly states that if we walk with God and are obedient to His Word, He promises to prolong our life. Because Enoch walked with God, God prolonged his days, and he was the first to experience something that no one else had experienced.

God 'took' Enoch.

Again, Genesis 5:24, says, "And Enoch walked with God: and he was not; for God *took* him." It seems that the close, intimate connection between Enoch and the Father was so special that the Father could not bear to leave him on the earth any longer — so He took Enoch into Heaven.

Here we have the first recorded *rapture* in the Bible! People today who mock the idea of the rapture of the Church don't know Scripture. Enoch's sudden "catching away" to be with God is a foreshadow and an example of what will happen to all believers who are alive at the time of Christ's return to gather the Church unto Himself (*see* 1 Thessalonians 4:15-17).

To be clear: Enoch never died. He is still alive in Heaven to this day, which means even though his son Methuselah lived to be 969 years and then died, Enoch outlived him. Miraculously, his physical body has been preserved in the glorious presence of God for about 5,000 years, making Enoch the longest man to ever live!

Enoch was translated and could not be found.

The life of Enoch is so fascinating that he is also mentioned in the New Testament. In what is often referred to as the "Hall of Faith" chapter in the book of Hebrews, Scripture says, "By faith Enoch was translated that he should not see death; and was not found, because God had translated him: for before his translation he had this testimony, that he pleased God" (Hebrews 11:5).

Notice that the words "translated" or "translation" appear three times in this one verse. In each instance, it is the Greek word *metatithimi*, which means *to translate* or *to transfer*. The repeated use of this word tells us that Enoch was most definitely *translated* or *transferred* out of this natural world and into Heaven. This was a supernatural transformation unlike any other.

Moreover, the writer of Hebrews specified that Enoch did *not* see death. The word "not" is the Greek word *ouch*, which means *emphatically not*. Enoch most emphatically did not experience death, and he "…was not found" (Hebrews 11:5). In Greek, the word "found" is *heurisko*, which means *to find* or *to discover*. It signifies *a discovery made as a result of careful observation; a moment when one makes a surprising or conclusive discovery*. The use of this word *heurisko* points to a discovery made due to an intense investigation, scientific study, or scholarly research.

So when the Bible says that Enoch "was not found," it is telling us that people were searching, looking, and investigating intensely, but they could most emphatically *not* find him. He disappeared from the face of the earth because God took him.

Enoch held tightly to the word God gave him.

One more thing to note about this passage is that it says, "…For before his translation he had this testimony, that he pleased God" (Hebrews 11:5). The word "before" is the Greek word *pro*, which means *earlier* and implies that Enoch had been given a "word" from God *earlier* in his life that he would never taste death, and Enoch held tightly to that word until God made it a reality.

God spoke to him, and he waited and waited. During the wait, he may have wondered, *Will this word ever come to pass?* Nevertheless, he continued to walk with God and stayed in faith. Then, finally, at the age of 365 years, that word became a reality in his life.

The Bible also says that Enoch had a "testimony." This word is a translation of the Greek word *martureo*, which describes *a testimony in a court of law.* It is the term from where we get the word *martyr*, which is *one who suffers unjustly for what he believes.* The use of this word implies that Enoch likely suffered skepticism and maybe even ridicule from those who heard him declare he would never die. But regardless of what he suffered, he didn't abandon the word God gave him, and his actions pleased the Lord.

Enoch is considered the first Old Testament prophet.

An interesting note about Enoch is that many Jews identify him as the first prophet in Scripture. In fact, he was so in sync with the Spirit of God that he was able to see thousands of years into the future and get a glimpse of Christ's Second Coming. This prophetic vision is recorded in Jude 14 and 15:

> **And Enoch also, the seventh from Adam, prophesied of these, saying, Behold, the Lord cometh with ten thousands of his saints, to execute judgment upon all, and to convince all that are ungodly among them of all their ungodly deeds which they have ungodly committed, and of all their hard speeches which ungodly sinners have spoken against him.**

Amazing! At the age of 365, Enoch was able to see nearly 5,000 years into the future — even beyond our present day — and prophesy the Lord's coming in the clouds with an untold number of His saints. It seems that after he and his wife became the parents of Methuselah when he was 65, something changed in his life, and it caused him to spend the next 300 years walking closer and closer with the Lord.

Enoch's life demonstrates that if you will align yourself with God and His Word, standing by it and refusing to retreat, a great reward is ahead for you. Realize that Enoch reached his peak of productivity at age 365 — that is when he had his greatest experience with God. So regardless of how old you are, you are never too old to be used of God and experience His marvelous salvation.

Friend, if God has made a promise to you that has not been fulfilled yet, it's not time for you to give up. It's time for you to press in, stay in faith, and say, "God, I'm not checking out. I'm not leaving this planet until I have seen the fulfillment of what You promised me." Your best season is not behind you — it's in front of you! Believe it and receive it, in Jesus' name!

STUDY QUESTIONS

Study to shew thyself approved unto God, a workman that needeth not to be ashamed, rightly dividing the word of truth.
— 2 Timothy 2:15

1. What stage of life are you in presently? According to the latest statistics, what stage or level of productivity should you be in? Does your personal experience line up with that? If it doesn't, pray and ask the Lord what you can do to see things improve.

2. The extremely long life lived by Enoch's son Methuselah demonstrates God's mercy. According to Ezekiel 33:11, how does God feel about punishing wicked, sinful people? What does Second Peter 3:9 say is the reason for what seems to be a delay in Him bringing judgment on our present-day, sinful society? Why do you think it is vital to keep these verses in mind?

PRACTICAL APPLICATION

But be ye doers of the word, and not hearers only, deceiving your own selves.
— James 1:22

1. Age is not a minus — it's a *plus*! More years of life means more time to mature, grow, and gain priceless experience. Looking back over your life, how is growing older given you greater understanding of how to walk with God, discern right from wrong, and have a better handle on what He has called you to do? What things do you now know, and what can you now do that you needed time to learn?

2. According to Hebrews 11:5, God had spoken to Enoch earlier and told him he would not taste death, and Enoch waited and waited until God's promise was fulfilled. What has God spoken to *you* by His Spirit? What promise are you waiting for Him to fulfill? How does Enoch's life inspire you with hope to believe God will do what He said?

TOPIC
Noah — Getting Started at 500 Years of Age

SCRIPTURES

1. **Psalm 91:16** — With long life will I satisfy him, and shew him my salvation.

2. **Genesis 5:28,29** — And Lamech lived an hundred eighty and two years, and begat a son: and he called his name Noah, saying, This same shall comfort us concerning our work and toil of our hands....

3. **Genesis 5:32** — And Noah was five hundred years old: and Noah begat Shem, Ham, and Japheth.

4. **Genesis 7:6** — And Noah was six hundred years old when the flood of waters was upon the earth.

5. **Hebrews 11:7** — By faith Noah, being warned of God of things not seen as yet, moved with fear, prepared an ark to the saving of his house....

GREEK WORDS

1. "being warned" — **χρηματίζω** (*chrematidzo*): a business transaction; to transact business; to advise or consult with one about important affairs; in this case, to be advised and consulted by God; literally, being divinely advised and warned

2. "not seen as yet" — **μηδέπω** (*medepo*): not yet or never before

3. "moved with fear" — **εὐλαβέομαι** (*eulabeomai*): to do something cautiously; to take action urgently and seriously

4. "prepared" — **κατασκευάζω** (*kataskeuadzo*): to put forth effort to build a vessel

5. "ark" — **κιβωτός** (*kibotos*): a ship, not only for sailing, but also for warehousing and saving

6. "to the saving of his house" — **εἰς σωτηρίαν τοῦ οἴκου αὐτοῦ** (*eis soterian tou oikou autou*): for the explicit purpose of saving his own household

SYNOPSIS

The giant redwoods are the tallest of trees in the world and are only found on the west coast from central California through southern Oregon. As we noted previously, these trees can live thousands of years, and with the right amount of water, redwoods can grow two to three feet in a year![1]

One of the most amazing places to see the finest of the redwoods is called Avenue of the Giants in Northern California. These trees are absolutely enormous! They reach hundreds of feet into the sky and are massive in size. You can even drive a car through three of them, and some of are more than 4,000 years old!

Symbolically, God wants to cultivate you into a spiritual redwood. He wants you to grow mighty and massive in Christ and live a very long, fruitful life. The Bible is filled with God's promises of longevity to those who love and obey Him. Enoch's life is an example. He walked with God and experienced his spiritual peak at 365 years of age! In this lesson, we will examine the life of Noah and see how God used him to save the world at the age of 600!

The emphasis of this lesson:

Noah began his greatest assignment for God at the age of 500. For 100 years, he and his family worked to accomplish God's will by building the ark. Being divinely warned of what was coming, Noah was moved with godly fear and obeyed the Lord, despite all questioning, criticism, and ridicule from others.

The Stats on Longevity Speak Volumes

Before we get into the life of Noah, let's quickly review the statistics from some of the latest scientific research on productivity among the aged. If you are 60, 65, 70, or even 80 and you think you are too old to do great things for God, think again!

Recent studies show that...

- The most productive age is from 60 to 70 years of age.
- The second most productive stage is from 70 to 80 years of age.
- The third most productive stage is from 50 to 60 years of age.

You may be wondering how it is possible to be so productive in your senior years. It is because the longer you live, the more knowledge and experience you gain. Thus, between the ages of 60 and 70, you are more prepared and equipped than ever to be more productive and to be a bigger blessing to others than at any other time in your life.

Even if you are between the ages of 70 and 80, you are still in the second most productive season of your life. If you're between the ages of 50 and 60, the time most people are thinking about retirement, you certainly need to work hard to prepare for your future, but don't be focused on heading for retirement. Your most productive years are just in front of you!

Sadly, when most people retire in their mid-60s, they have few if any relationships, and they tend to sit around and focus on the aches and pains in their body because they don't have anything else to do. Some individuals even get sick and die early because they feel their life no longer has purpose since they're not working.

Don't let that be your story. Change the way you are thinking!

The average age of Nobel Prize winners is late 60s to early 70s. What if these individuals had retired early? They would have probably missed this remarkable achievement. Statistics also tell us:

- The average age of presidents of prominent companies is 57 to 60 years.
- The average age of pastors of the 100 largest churches in the U.S. is 71 years.
- The average age of those who become Popes is 78 years.

The fact is that the best years of your life are between 60 and 80 years of age. At age 60, you begin to reach your potential, and this continues into your 80s. If you are between 60 and 70 years of age, you are in the best mental level of your life; and if you are 70-80, you are in the second-best mental level of your life.

For the first 30 years of your life, you are focused on *learning*. During the second 30 years, you are focused on *working* and *doing*. And the third 30 years of your life should be spent on *imparting to others* and helping them get started and move forward in their life's calling, which means we need to plan to live *at least* 90 years.

God Wants To Satisfy You
With Long Life

In Psalm 91:16, God said, "With long life will I satisfy him, and shew him my salvation." Notice it doesn't say you're going to get old, become broken down, and shrivel up and die." It says that God will satisfy you with long life and show you His salvation.

The use of the word "show" in this verse is the equivalent of God saying, "I want to demonstrate My salvation to you in your older years." And that word "salvation" describes the full package of God's blessings. It includes health and a healthy body, sound thinking or a sound mind, and prosperity and success. God wants you to experience every bit of His goodness to the very end of your life. His desire is to make you a trophy of His grace and His power.

At the beginning of Psalm 91:16, God says, "With long life will I satisfy him…." The word "long" in Hebrew speaks of *length of days* or *longevity*. The word "life" in Hebrew speaks of *days*. Together as a phrase, "long life" depicts *long days* or *a very long life*. Hence, you could translate this verse, "With a very, very long life will I satisfy him."

That brings us to the word "satisfy," which means *to have enough*, *to have plenty of*, or *to be fully satisfied*. God promises you that you will live until you're *satisfied*, and you don't have to leave planet earth until you're ready to go. But this promise comes with conditions, which are found in Psalm 91:1: "He that dwelleth in the secret place of the most High shall abide under the shadow of the Almighty." You must dwell in His secret place and in His shadow.

Although some may think this is a fairytale, it is not. This is God's own Word and what He promises in Psalm 91:16. If you are struggling to believe it, you are thinking wrong, and you need to renew your mind to the truth.

If you aim for a longer life, you'll come closer to it. But if you just believe for 70 or 80 years, that's probably all you will get. It's time you raise your level of faith and begin to declare that you will aim for the maximum number of years and live until you are fully satisfied. If you believe for it, God will show you His salvation and provide you with strength, health, a sharp mind, and prosperity.

Noah Was Birthed
To Bring the World Comfort and Rest

In Lesson 2, we looked at Enoch and saw that he lived on the earth to be 365 years old, which was really when he hit his peak. At the age of 365, he was closer to God and experienced the fulfillment of the promise God made to him — that he would not taste death.

We also learned that Enoch had a son whose name was Methuselah. And if you study Adam's genealogy in Genesis 5, you will discover that at the age of 187, Methuselah fathered a son named Lamech (v. 26). When Lamech was 182, he had a son whom he named Noah. The first appearance of Noah is in Genesis 5:28 and 29, which says:

> **And Lamech lived an hundred eighty and two years, and begat a son: and he called his name Noah, saying, This same shall comfort us concerning our work and toil of our hands....**

In Hebrew, the name "Noah" means *comfort* or *rest*. Lamech gave Noah such a name because he received divine revelation that this was a special son whom God would use to play a prophetic role in humanity. Through Noah, the world would finally receive comfort and rest from all the dark, nefarious activities that had been occurring.

In the time before the Flood, Genesis 6 records that the sons of God (angels) abandoned their God-given place of authority and came into the earth to mate with women. As a result, they spawned a race of hybrid beings called Nephilim, or giants. For an in-depth look at what was happening in the world at the time of Noah, we recommend you check out Rick's book *Fallen Angels, Giants, Monsters and the World Before the Flood*.

At the Age of 500,
Noah Began His Work for God

The Bible is silent about the first five hundred years of Noah's life. Then in Genesis 5:32 we read, "And Noah was five hundred years old: and Noah begat Shem, Ham, and Japheth." How would you like to become a new parent and start a family at the age of 500? That's what Noah and his wife did, and it seems it was about that same time that God began to speak to Noah directly.

For generations, God had been talking to the people in Noah's family line, including his father Lamech, his grandfather Methuselah, his great-grandfather Enoch, and his great-great-grandfather Jared. Thus, Noah had likely heard again and again that a judgement was coming, and that Methuselah's death would trigger that judgment.

For years, Noah carried within him all the prophetic words and warnings that had been passed to him from his father, his grandfather, his great-grandfather, his great-great-grandfather. This shows us two important things: First, we should treasure the words of faithful family members who have walked with God before us. Second, as we get older, we have a God-given responsibility to pass on to the upcoming generations the knowledge and wisdom of what we've learned.

When Noah reached the age of 500 and became a father, suddenly, he had a spiritual awakening and began to hear from God for himself.

In the same way, there are some things you will not hear from God until you get to an older age. As time passes and you mature, you become more primed and prepared to hear what the Spirit of God wants to say to you. That's what seems to have happened with Noah.

When God began speaking with Noah directly, He instructed Noah to begin building the Ark (*see* Genesis 6:13-22). The project took nearly 100 years for Noah and his family to complete. Then, at the age of 600, the Flood came on the earth. Genesis 7:6 says, "And Noah was six hundred years old when the flood of waters was upon the earth."

God Warned Noah of 'Things Not Yet Seen'

Like Enoch, Noah is also mentioned in the Hebrews 11 "Hall of Faith." In verse 7, the Bible says, "By faith Noah, being warned of God of things not seen as yet, moved with fear, prepared an ark to the saving of his house...."

Notice the phrase "being warned." It is a translation of the Greek word *chrematidzo*, which describes *a business transaction*. That is the way Noah viewed His interaction with God — as a business relationship in which God was the senior partner and Noah was the junior partner. Hence, the word *chrematidzo* means *to transact business* or *to advise or consult with one about important affairs.* In Noah's case, he was literally being divinely advised by God and warned of things *not yet seen.*

The words "not seen as yet" are derived from the Greek word *medepo,* which means *not yet* or *never before.* The use of this word makes total sense when we realize that God advised and warned Noah about a worldwide flood that he and no one else had never seen before. In fact, no one had even seen rain.

The Bible says in Genesis 2:5 and 6 that from the time of Creation to the Flood, the vegetation was watered by a mist that came up from the ground. So there had never been rain — much less a *flood.* Yet that is what Noah was being divinely warned was coming.

'Moved with Fear,' Noah 'Prepared an Ark'

Building an ark was a massive task that took massive faith. The Bible even says that when God told Noah what was coming, he was "moved with fear." In Greek, this is the word *eulabeomai,* and it means *to do something cautiously* or *to take action urgently and seriously.* The use of this word indicates that Noah knew he had heard from God, and he was quick to obey. He was not afraid for himself; he simply had a sense of awe and responsibility to do as he had been instructed.

In response to God's warning and instructions, Noah "…prepared an ark to the saving of his house…" (Hebrews 11:7). The word "prepared" here is the Greek word *kataskeuadzo,* which means *to put forth effort to build a vessel.* Noah put forth everything he had into the construction of the ark, building it exactly according to the plan God had given him.

The word "ark" in Greek is *kibotos,* and it describes *an ancient ship that was not only for sailing but was also for warehousing and saving.* As you read Genesis 7, you will see that God instructed Noah to take with him on the ark a male and female of every kind of land animal and bird. Certain animals that were classified as *clean* and to be used as sacrificial offerings he was to take seven pairs.

The Bible says that when the ark was finished and God told Noah to get on board, "Pairs of all creatures that have the breath of life in them *came to Noah and entered the ark.* The animals going in were male and female of every living thing, as God had commanded Noah. Then the Lord shut him in" (Genesis 7:15,16 *NIV*). Amazingly, God moved on the animals, and they instinctively came to Noah and got on the ark. Once the Flood was over, they would disembark from the ark and repopulate the post-flood world.

Every obedient action Noah did was "to the saving of his house." In the original Greek, this phrase literally means *for the explicit purpose of saving his own household.*

It's Almost Certain That Noah Was Questioned, Criticized, and Ridiculed by Others

The Ark's construction took 100 years, and more than likely, there were many challenging moments for Noah to navigate. Perhaps there were times when his wife asked, "Are you absolutely sure that God has spoken to you? People are laughing at us. We're investing every moment of our lives and all our resources to build this ark. Our sons and their wives are doing the same. Are you really sure God spoke to you?" Her questioning may have been a strong tug on Noah's heart and mind to give up and to stop the project.

Or how about his sons? They could have said, "Dad, we're giving our whole life, our future, and our reputation for this project. Are you sure you've heard from God?" Those kinds of words would have surely given Noah an opportunity to second-guess himself and abandon the assignment God had given him.

It is also very likely that the people in the community laughed at him and his family, saying things like, "What's wrong with that old man? He started building a big boat in front of his house at age 500, and he's been at it for 100 years! He keeps talking about rain and something called a 'flood' that's coming. Is he out of his mind?"

It is safe to say many mocked Noah and his sons and made fun of them repeatedly. They probably made up all kinds of nasty, derogatory jokes about him and his family. Was he tempted to give up the project? It's almost a certainty. There were forces all around him, pulling on him and trying to move him out of his place of faith. But Noah knew he had heard from God and refused to abandon the project.

But the Bible says that instead of quitting, Noah became "a preacher of righteousness" (*see* 2 Peter 2:5), which means that along with building the ark, he was also telling people to repent because a worldwide flood was coming, and it would destroy the earth and everything in it. Regardless of any criticism or questions from his family — or personal concerns that weighed on his mind — Noah stayed in faith and completed his assignment.

Age Is Meant To Prepare You For What God Wants You To Do

Noah had a spiritual awakening at age 500 and began to hear from God for himself. Likewise, it is during *your* senior years that you are (or will be) in need of a spiritual awakening. Your senior years are not the time to pack up and head off the field. Instead, it is time to really hear from God and receive the most important assignment of your life.

At age 500, Noah was finally ready to do what God had called him to do. He had the wisdom, the resources, and the needed experience to accomplish God's will. In the same way, when you reach the latter years of your life, you are more primed and prepared for a new assignment than at any other time in your life.

So if you are older, it is a great time to start a new project that God has put on your heart! You're more equipped and wiser now. Indeed, the days and years directly in front of you should be the greatest fruit-producing season of your life. But to see it happen, you must reach out by faith and embrace what God is asking you to do and begin to declare, "The last part of my life is going to be the greatest season of all! I'm not leaving this world until I've done *all* that God has called me to do!"

STUDY QUESTIONS

Study to shew thyself approved unto God, a workman that needeth not to be ashamed, rightly dividing the word of truth. — 2 Timothy 2:15

1. The Bible says that once Noah heard from God, he was "moved with fear" and quickly obeyed. Consider your own life. When God gives you instruction, are you quick to obey or slow in responding? What is the very last thing you remember the Holy Spirit prompting you to do? Did you do it? If not, repent for your delay, and get it done

today. If so, do you know what God is asking you to do in this current season? Be prompt to obey!

2. Clearly, Noah had a healthy, reverential *fear of the Lord*, which means he had a deep sense of awe and respect for God as the Supreme Authority and All-Powerful One. What do you know about the fear of the Lord? Here are a few important truths from Scripture you need to know:

   - **What is the fear of the Lord?** Psalm 33:8; 34:11-14; Proverbs 8:13
   - **The fear of the Lord is wisdom**: Psalm 111:10; Proverbs 1:7; 2:5; 9:10; 15:33
   - **The fear of the Lord brings protection**: Psalm 33:18; 34:7;
   - **The fear of the Lord helps us stay away from evil:** Psalm 103:17; Proverbs 16:6
   - **The fear of the Lord unveils secrets and yields honor and riches:** Psalm 25:14; Proverbs 22:4
   - **The fear of the Lord provides life and longevity**: Proverbs 10:27; 14:27; 19:23

PRACTICAL APPLICATION

**But be ye doers of the word, and not hearers only,
deceiving your own selves.
—James 1:22**

1. At the age of 500, Noah became a father and had a spiritual awakening. For the first time, he began to hear from God for himself. Can you remember the first time you really began to hear the voice of God's Spirit? How old were you and what was going on in your life? What did He speak to you?

2. Noah carried within him all the prophetic words and warnings that had been passed to him from his older family members. What God-lessons, wisdom, and prophetic words have been passed on to you by your God-fearing family members, mentors, and friends? How have these priceless treasures shaped and impacted your life?

3. As you grow older, you have a God-given responsibility to pass on the knowledge you have learned to the younger, upcoming generations. What godly wisdom and spiritual insights are you passing on to your

children, grandchildren, nieces, and nephews? What is one thing you wish someone would have told you that you can share with others?

---

(1) Giant Sequoias and Redwoods: The Largest and Tallest of Trees (https://www.livescience.com/39461-sequoias-redwood-trees.html; accessed 12/4/24).

TOPIC

Abraham — A Late Start at 75 Years of Age

SCRIPTURES

1. **Genesis 12:1-4** — Now the Lord had said unto Abram, Get thee out of thy country, and from thy kindred, and from thy father's house, unto a land that I will shew thee: and I will make of thee a great nation, and I will bless thee, and make thy name great; and thou shalt be a blessing: and I will bless them that bless thee, and curse him that curseth thee: and in thee shall all families of the earth be blessed. So Abram departed, as the Lord had spoken unto him....

2. **Acts 7:2,3** — And he said, Men, brethren, and fathers, hearken; The God of glory appeared unto our father Abraham, when he was in Mesopotamia, before he dwelt in Charran, and said unto him, Get thee out of thy country, and from thy kindred, and come into the land which I shall shew thee.

3. **Galatians 3:8** — And the scripture, foreseeing that God would justify the heathen through faith, preached before the gospel unto Abraham, saying, In thee shall all nations be blessed.

4. **Hebrews 11:8,9** — By faith Abraham, when he was called to go out into a place which he should after receive for an inheritance, obeyed; and he went out, not knowing whither he went. By faith he sojourned in the land of promise, as in a strange country, dwelling in tabernacles with Isaac and Jacob, the heirs with him of the same promise.

GREEK WORDS

1. "called" — **καλούμενος** (*kaloumenos*): literally, being called; to call, to invite, or to summon; depicts a summoning that requires the hearer to respond

2. "place" — **τόπος** (*topos*): a real geographical location

3. "receive" — **λαμβάνω** (*lambano*): to receive into one's possession; to take into one's own control and ownership; carries the idea of taking hold of something, grasping onto something, and embracing it so tightly that it becomes your very own

4. "obeyed" — **ὑπακούω** (*hupakouo*): a compound of **ὑπό** (*hupo*) and **ἀκούω** (*akouo*); the word **ὑπό** (*hupo*) means under or by, and the word **ἀκούω** (*akouo*) means I hear; compounded, it pictures one in a sub-servient position who hears and obeys what is being said to him by a superior; being under authority, listening, and carrying out instructions

5. "not knowing" — **μὴ ἐπιστάμενος** (*me epistamenos*): the word **μὴ** (*me*) means not, and **ἐπιστάμενος** (*epistamenos*) depicts one who is on top of his subject, one who possesses professional knowledge, or one who is highly skilled and knowledgeable; in this case, because of the added **μὴ** (*me*), it is one who is unacquainted, unknowledgeable, unskilled, and unprofessional in where he is going and in what he is doing

6. "whither he went" — **ποῦ ἔρχεται** (*pou erchetai*): where he was going; where he was headed

7. "sojourned" — **παροικέω** (*paroikeo*): to live outside the house; figuratively, to live on the street

8. "strange country" — **ἀλλότριος** (*allotrios*): alien; foreign; strange; unfamiliar; unnatural and even a bit weird

9. "dwelling" — **κατοικέω** (*katoikeo*): settling down into a home; describes a permanent resident

10. "tabernacles" — **σκηνή** (*skene*): tents

SYNOPSIS

Hopefully, you are beginning to see just how important it is for you to embrace the fact that God is all about you living a long life and being fruitful in your senior years. If you are younger, you should be aware of this truth so that your thinking lines up with God's Word and you are learning and preparing for the years ahead.

If you're already a senior, make sure that you understand that your latter years are the best years of your life, and if you have not thought that way, you must renew your mind and adjust your thinking to this aspect of God's will. You're not supposed to fade from the scene and die an old, sick person. On the contrary, God wants you to go from *glory to glory* and *strength to strength* (*see* Psalm 84:7; 2 Corinthians 3:18).

In this lesson, we will look at Abraham, the father of faith and see that even though he got a late start in life, it did not hinder him from accomplishing unprecedented things for God.

The emphasis of this lesson:

God first appeared to Abraham when he was 75 years of age, engulfing him in His glorious presence. Abraham accepted God's invitation, submitted to God's authority, and obeyed what He said, not having a clue what God was asking him to do or where he was to go.

Our Greatest Years
Are Our Latter Years

As we have noted in our previous lessons, there are encouraging statistics regarding the latter years of our life. New studies show that…

- The most productive age is from 60 to 70 years of age.
- The second most productive stage is from 70 to 80 years of age.
- The third most productive stage is from 50 to 60 years of age.

So when multitudes of people are thinking about heading for retirement between the ages of 50 and 60, they really should be thinking about how to utilize the greatest, most productive season of their life, which is right in front of them.

- The average age of Nobel Prize winners is late 60s to early 70s.
- The average age of presidents of prominent companies is 57 to 60 years.
- The average age of pastors of the 100 largest churches in the U.S. is 71 years.
- The average age of individuals who become Popes is 78 years.

Friend, the best years of your life are between the ages of 60 and 80. At age 60, you begin to reach your potential, and this continues into your 80s. If you're between the ages of 60 and 70, you're in the best mental level of your life! And if you are between the ages of 70 and 80, you are in the second-best mental level of your life.

If you think about it, by the time you reach 60, you've been around long enough that you know the right things to do and what things to avoid. You also know what you want and what you don't want out of life. You're able to make decisions faster because you have a greater base of information, knowledge, and experience.

In your first 30 years of life, you *learn*. In the second 30 years, you are *working* and *doing*. And in the third 30 years, you invest time *imparting to and helping* others.

To Experience High Productivity, We Must Take Care of Our Body

Of course, the only way you will experience the highest levels of productivity in your senior years is if you've taken care of your body all the years before that. The Bible tells us in First Thessalonians 4:4, "…That every one of you should know how to possess his vessel in sanctification and honour."

The word "vessel" here refers to one's *body*. To "possess your vessel in sanctification and honor" means you're taking care of your body and using your mind. This includes eating right, exercising, and continuing to grow as a person by learning and cultivating healthy relationships with godly people. If you're "possessing your vessel," you should be able to experience the wonderful above-mentioned statistics.

Think about the tools and instruments in your garage. Although it is basically a controlled environment with consistent conditions, if the tools and instruments are not used, they can begin to rust and eventually become inoperable. The only way that an instrument remains usable is by *using* it.

The same is true with your body. If you eat the wrong food, your body can become sick and toxic. Likewise, if you don't move your body regularly, your blood and tissues will become stagnant and deteriorate. That's why Paul said, "That every one of you should know how to possess his vessel in sanctification and honour" (1 Thessalonians 4:4).

Friend, you must treat your body well and with honor because it is the only one you get, and it is special! Scripture says, "…Don't you realize that your body is the temple of the Holy Spirit, who lives in you and was given to you by God? You do not belong to yourself" (1 Corinthians 6:19 *NLT*). So be sure to move your body and use your mind. Develop yourself through reading, studying, and memorization. If you use the instrument God gave you, and take good care if it, it will last a lifetime.

The Details of God's Call to Abraham Are Found in the Old and New Testament

As we mentioned in Lesson 1, Abraham is often referred to as the father of faith. When God first called him, he was known as Abram and was already 75 years of age. His story first appears in Genesis 12:

> **Now the Lord had said unto Abram, Get thee out of thy country, and from thy kindred, and from thy father's house, unto a land that I will shew thee: And I will make of thee a great nation, and I will bless thee, and make thy name great; and thou shalt be a blessing: And I will bless them that bless thee, and curse him that curseth thee: and in thee shall all families of the earth be blessed. So Abram departed, as the Lord had spoken unto him; and Lot went with him: and Abram was seventy and five years old when he departed out of Haran….**
> **— Genesis 12:1-4**

At that time, Abraham and his wife, Sarah, were living in Ur of the Chaldees, which was one of the most prosperous and luxurious areas in the world. Thus, Abraham was a rich man and well-established with a great reputation, and now God was telling him to leave it all at age 75.

Abraham experienced the glory of God.

What is interesting is that the call of Abraham is also mentioned in Acts 7, and it includes additional information that is not found in Genesis. Stephen, who was one of the leaders in the Early Church, was speaking to the Jewish leaders and retelling what happened with Abraham:

> **And he said, Men, brethren, and fathers, hearken; The God of glory appeared unto our father Abraham, when he was in Mesopotamia, before he dwelt in Charran, and said unto him,**

> **Get thee out of thy country, and from thy kindred, and come into the land which I shall shew thee.**
>
> — Acts 7:2,3

According to this verse, the glory of God "appeared" to Abraham before he lived in Harran. In Greek, the word "appeared" depicts Abraham being *enshrouded in a cloud of God's glory*. There he was, a pagan, living in the land of Ur of the Chaldeans, worshiping the moon. Then one day, God suddenly "appeared" to him, enshrouding him in a glorious cloud of His presence.

Abraham was the first to hear the Gospel.

God not only gave Abraham the assignment for his life, but He also announced to him the message of the Gospel. We find this detail in Galatians 3:8, where the Bible says:

> **And the scripture, foreseeing that God would justify the heathen through faith, preached before the gospel unto Abraham, saying, In thee shall all nations be blessed.**

Thus, Abraham was the first man in all of history to hear the Gospel, and he heard it through God's own voice booming out of a cloud of glory!

When Abraham was called, he accepted God's invitation.

Like Enoch and Noah, Abraham is also mentioned in the Hebrews "Hall of Faith" chapter. In this New Testament book, there are details the writer of Hebrews included that are not anywhere else in Scripture. Hebrews 11:8 says:

> **By faith Abraham, when he was called to go out into a place which he should after receive for an inheritance, obeyed; and he went out, not knowing whither he went.**

This verse is *packed* with meaning, so let's look at the original Greek text to see what the Holy Spirit is telling us.

First, notice it says, "By faith Abraham, when he was called...." The word "called" in Greek is *kaloumenos*, which literally means, *being called; to call, to invite*, or *to summon*. The use of this word tells us that God gave Abraham an invitation that he could either accept or reject. This was a summoning that required the hearer to respond. Thus, at age 75, Abraham was a called man, and when he received God's call, he received a supernatural revelation or enlightenment that his life had a specific purpose.

By faith, Abraham actively took ownership of what God had for him.

Hebrews 11:8 then adds that Abaham "…was called to go out into a place," and the word "place" is the Greek word *topos*, which is where we get the idea of *a topographical map*, and it describes *a real geographical location*. When Abraham heard God speaking to him, he knew he needed to get into the right *place*.

The verse continues, "…which he should after receive for an inheritance…." The word "receive" is important. It is a form of the Greek word *lambano*, and it means *to receive into one's possession* or *to take into one's own control and ownership*. This word carries the idea of taking hold of something, grasping onto something, and embracing it so tightly that it becomes your very own.

The use of the word *lambano* here means that by faith, Abraham said, "I'm going to take ownership of what God has said to me." He couldn't be passive; he had to be *actively involved* in engaging his faith. Abraham was grasping onto every word, embracing each one tightly, until this calling literally became his very own.

Similarly, whether you are young or older, you must reach out by faith, engage your faith, and embrace what God is offering you. You must take it and take ownership of it, just as Abraham did!

Abraham heard and obeyed what the Lord said.

Again, Hebrews 11:8 says, "By faith Abraham, when he was called to go out into a place which he should after receive for an inheritance, obeyed; and he went out, not knowing whither he went."

Take note of the word "obeyed." It is the marvelous Greek word *hupakouo*, a compound of *hupo* and *akouo*. The word *hupo* means *under* or *by*, and the word *akouo* means *I hear*. It is where we get the English word *acoustics*. When these words are compounded to form *hupakouo*, the new word pictures *one in a subservient position who hears and obeys what is being said to him by a superior*.

Moreover, *hupakouo* depicts *being under authority* or *listening and carrying out instructions*. The use of the word *hupakouo* — translated in this verse as "obeyed"— lets us know that Abraham first listened to God and then submitted to His authority, carrying out His instructions. Hence, the moment Abraham came under God's authority, God became the Lord of Abraham's life.

Abraham opened his ears to hear and made a decision that he was going to obey. Likewise, that is what happens when *you* call Jesus the Lord of your life. You suddenly take on a subservient position (*hupo*) under Jesus, and He becomes your Lord. In that position, your job is to have your ears open to hear whatever He is saying to you, and from that point forward, your task in life is to say, "Yes, sir," and obey Him.

Abraham was unacquainted and unknowledgeable of what God asked him to do.

Once Abraham made the decision to obey God, the Bible says, "…he went out, not knowing whither he went" (Hebrews 11:8). The phrase "not knowing" in Greek is *me epistamenos*. The word *me* means *not*, and *epistamenos* depicts *one who is on top of his subject, one who possesses professional knowledge*, or *one who is highly skilled and knowledgeable*.

In this case, because the little Greek word *me* is in front of *epistamenos*, it cancels the meaning. Thus, *me epistamenos* — translated here as "not knowing" — depicts *one who is unacquainted, unknowledgeable, unskilled*, and *unprofessional in where he is going and in what he is doing*. The use of this word means God was asking Abraham to do something in which he had no previous experience. He was unskilled, unacquainted, unknowledgeable, and had no clue about what God was calling him to do or how to do it.

Specifically, this verse says Abraham went out "…not knowing whither he went" (Hebrews 11:8). The phrase "whither he went" is a translation of the Greek words *pou erchetai*, and it means *where he was going* or *where he was headed*.

Abraham lived in tents in a strange land for 100 years.

In the very next verse, the writer continued revealing to us Abraham's response of obedience, telling us, "By faith he sojourned in the land of promise, as in a strange country, dwelling in tabernacles with Isaac and Jacob, the heirs with him of the same promise" (Hebrews 11:9).

The word "sojourned" in this verse is the Greek word *paroikeo*, which means *to live outside the house; figuratively, to live on the street*. So when the Bible says, "By faith he sojourned," it means Abraham left his beautiful house in Ur of the Chaldees and began to live on the street "…in the land of promise, as in a strange country…" (Hebrews 11:9).

In Greek, the phrase "strange country" is *allotrios*, and it describes *something alien, foreign, strange, unfamiliar, unnatural* and even a bit *weird*. Abraham relocated to a territory with which he was completely *unfamiliar* and in his eyes was *alien, foreign, unnatural*, and even a bit *weird*. It was in this strange land that he was like a nomad or a vagabond "dwelling in tabernacles."

The word "dwelling" is *katoikeo* in Greek, and it means *settling down into a home*. It describes a person who settles into a permanent residence. The word "tabernacles" — the Greek word *skene* — is the term for *tents*. Hence, after Abraham spent 75 years in Ur, God appeared to Abraham and called him to leave everything connected with his life of luxury and begin living a vastly different life in a foreign country.

Despite challenges and personal doubts, Abraham remained committed to God's call.

Genesis 25:7 tells us that Abraham lived 175 years, which means for the remaining 100 years of his life, he was living in tents. It is certainly possible that as he wandered around, waiting to inherit the Promised Land, he had thoughts about returning to his luxurious life in Mesopotamia.

Perhaps his wife Sarah asked him a time or two, "Are you sure you heard from God? Back in Ur, we were living at ease, and now we're drifters with no place to call home. Do you really think God wants us to keep doing this?"

Yet despite the great famines, harsh desert conditions, and wars with enemies, Abraham *knew* he had heard from God, so he submitted himself to God's authority and refused to walk away from the great reward God had promised him.

Friend, you are called by God to get into agreement with Him and walk in faith, whether you're young, middle aged, or living in your senior years. Don't give up and move out of your divine assignment. When you are outside of the place God has called you — or *without faith* — it is impossible to please God (*see* Hebrews 11:6). But if you, like Abraham, will stay where God has called you to stay, do what God has told you to do, believe what He has told you to believe, and refuse to budge from it, payday will come!

STUDY QUESTIONS

**Study to shew thyself approved unto God, a workman that
needeth not to be ashamed, rightly dividing the word of truth.
— 2 Timothy 2:15**

1. Did you know that there were references about Abraham's life in
   Genesis, Acts, Galatians, and Hebrews? What facts about his life and
   his tenacious commitment to obey God were new to you? What was
   most intriguing about his response to the Lord's call?
2. The Bible talks about the life of Abraham in other books of the Bible as
   well, including Romans 4. Take some time to carefully read through this
   chapter and write down anything the Holy Spirit reveals to you about
   faith, righteousness, and our celebrated "father of faith," Abraham.
3. Scripture says that by faith, Abraham received, or *took personal ownership of,* what God had said to him. Rather than be passive, he was
   actively involved in engaging his faith. Consider your own life. Are
   you actively exercising your faith and taking ownership of what God
   has spoken to you? If so, what aspects of your life demonstrate your
   obedience to God and that you are actively engaging your faith to
   trust Him?

PRACTICAL APPLICATION

**But be ye doers of the word, and not hearers only,
deceiving your own selves.
— James 1:22**

1. To really experience the blessing of longevity and productivity in your
   senior years, you have to take care of your whole being — spirit, soul,
   and body. How are you treating your body? Do you see it as the home
   of the Holy Spirit? Are you honoring God with how and what you
   eat, and are you keeping your body in shape to the best of your ability?
   What changes do you recognize that the Lord is asking you to make
   to better "possess your vessel with honor and sanctification?"
2. Read First Thessalonians 4:4. Who in your life serves as an example
   of someone running a long race and is still going strong and serving
   robustly in his or her senior years? In what ways are you inspired to
   set a new standard to follow? What is it about this person that infuses

you with hope that with God's grace, you, too, can live a long, healthy, vibrant life?

TOPIC

Sarah — A Mother at 90 Years of Age

SCRIPTURES

1. **Genesis 17:1-6** — And when Abram was ninety years old and nine, the Lord appeared to Abram, and said unto him, I am the Almighty God; walk before me, and be thou perfect. And I will make my covenant between me and thee, and will multiply thee exceedingly. And Abram fell on his face: and God talked with him, saying, As for me, behold, my covenant is with thee, and thou shalt be a father of many nations. Neither shall thy name any more be called Abram, but thy name shall be Abraham; for a father of many nations have I made thee. And I will make thee exceeding fruitful, and I will make nations of thee, and kings shall come out of thee.

2. **Genesis 17:15-19** — And God said unto Abraham, As for Sarai thy wife, thou shalt not call her name Sarai, but Sarah shall her name be. And I will bless her, and give thee a son also of her: yea, I will bless her, and she shall be a mother of nations; kings of people shall be of her. Then Abraham fell upon his face, and laughed, and said in his heart, Shall a child be born unto him that is an hundred years old? and shall Sarah, that is ninety years old, bear? And Abraham said unto God, O that Ishmael might live before thee! And God said, Sarah thy wife shall bear thee a son indeed; and thou shalt call his name Isaac: and I will establish my covenant with him for an everlasting covenant, and with his seed after him.

3. **Genesis 17:21-22** — But my covenant will I establish with Isaac, which Sarah shall bear unto thee at this set time in the next year. And he left off talking with him, and God went up from Abraham.

4. **Genesis 18:9-15** — Now Abraham and Sarah were old and well stricken in age; and it ceased to be with Sarah after the manner of women. Therefore Sarah laughed within herself, saying, After I

am waxed old shall I have pleasure, my lord being old also? And the Lord said unto Abraham, Wherefore did Sarah laugh, saying, Shall I of a surety bear a child, which am old? Is any thing too hard for the Lord? At the time appointed I will return unto thee, according to the time of life, and Sarah shall have a son. Then Sarah denied, saying, I laughed not; for she was afraid. And he said, Nay; but thou didst laugh.

5. **Genesis 21:1-7** — And the Lord visited Sarah as he had said, and the Lord did unto Sarah as he had spoken. For Sarah conceived, and bare Abraham a son in his old age, at the set time of which God had spoken to him. And Abraham called the name of his son that was born unto him, whom Sarah bare to him, Isaac. And Abraham circumcised his son Isaac being eight days old, as God had commanded him. And Abraham was an hundred years old, when his son Isaac was born unto him. And Sarah said, God hath made me to laugh, so that all that hear will laugh with me. And she said, Who would have said unto Abraham, that Sarah should have given children suck? for I have born him a son in his old age.

6. **Hebrews 11:11,12** — Through faith also Sara herself received strength to conceive seed, and was delivered of a child when she was past age, because she judged him faithful who had promised. Therefore sprang there even of one, and him as good as dead, so many as the stars of the sky in multitude, and as the sand which is by the sea shore innumerable.

GREEK WORDS

1. "being barren" — **στεῖρος** (*steiros*): barren; sterile; unable to produce children

2. "received" — **λαμβάνω** (*lambano*): to receive into one's possession; to take into one's own control and ownership; carries the idea of taking hold of something, grasping onto something, and embracing it so tightly that it becomes your very own

3. "strength" — **δύναμις** (*dunamis*): power; it carries the idea of explosive, superhuman power that comes with enormous energy and produces phenomenal, extraordinary, and unparalleled results

4. "conceive" — **καταβολή** (*katabole*): hurling down; something forcibly put in place

5. "seed" — **σπέρμα** (*sperma*): seed; sperm

6. "when she was past age"— **καὶ παρὰ καιρὸν ἡλικίας** (*kai para kairon helikias*): even well beyond a suitable age; beyond the years of opportunity

7. "judged"— **ἡγέομαι** (*hegeomai*): to deem or to consider

8. "faithful"— **πιστὸν** (*piston*): absolutely faithful; absolutely trustworthy

9. "who had promised"— **τὸν ἐπαγγειλάμενον** (*ton epangeilamenon*): the one declaring and promising; depicts the declarer and promiser

SYNOPSIS

Many believers ask the question, "What is God's will for my life?" If that's you, here is one thing God definitely wants for you: He desires to see you grow spiritually and to see you transformed into the image of Jesus from one degree of glory to the next (*see* 2 Corinthians 3:18). Rather than go from strength to weakness and then die old and broken, His plan is for you to improve with age — moving from strength to strength and finishing your journey in a blaze of glory.

Sarah, Abraham's cherished wife, seems to have done just that. Even though God's promise of conceiving and birthing a child at age 90 seemed hysterically impossible, she chose to engage her faith and believe the word He had spoken, which is exactly what He wants us to do with what He has promised us.

The emphasis of this lesson:

God promised Sarah she would have a child at age 90 — when she was sterile and well beyond child-bearing age. Sarah engaged her faith and believed she would conceive, judging God to be absolutely faithful to His word. And God made good on His promise!

Our Senior Years
Are Our Most Productive Years

Without question, it is God's will for us to be fruitful with our lives all the way into our closing years. The Bible declares, "Those who are planted in the house of the Lord shall flourish in the courts of our God. They shall still bear fruit in old age…" (Psalm 92:13,14 *NKJV*). Recent studies show that…

- The most productive age is from 60 to 70 years of age.

- The second most productive stage is from 70 to 80 years of age.
- The third most productive stage is from 50 to 60 years of age.

Also keep in mind that...

- The average age of Nobel Prize winners is late 60s to early 70s.
- The average age of presidents of major companies is 57 to 60 years.
- The average age of pastors of the 100 largest churches in the U.S. is 71 years.
- The average age of individuals who become Popes is 78 years.

According to the above stats, the best years of your life are between the ages of 60 and 80. At age 60, you begin to reach your potential, and that continues developing into your 80s.

If you're young, you may be thinking, *This doesn't apply to me.* But while you may be young now, time is passing quickly. One day, should the Lord tarry, you will reach your senior years, and if you renew your thinking now, you will be ready to achieve all that you can in the most productive years of your life.

If you are a senior citizen and you're thinking, *Life is over, and I am no longer relevant,* change your thinking! If you're between the ages of 60 and 70, you are in the best mental capacity of your life, and if you are between the ages of 70 and 80, you are in the second-best mental capacity of your life. It makes sense that if you have used your mind throughout your life, it is filled with information. You are now primed and prepared to make the best decisions, knowing what to do and what not to do.

Your senior years are called your *golden years* because they are to be the most fruitful and enjoyable of all. During your first 30 years of life, you *learn*. In your second 30 years, you're actively *doing*. And in your third 30 years of life, you are focused on *imparting* and *helping* others.

Friend, God promises longevity for those who love and obey Him. Your most productive years are just ahead — even secular statistics prove that. So if you're among those who are older, it's not the time for you to retire and ride off into the sunset. Rather, it's time for you to embrace the most productive season of your life! Your best is yet to come!

A Life-Changing, Name-Altering
Encounter With God

To understand Sarah's story, we must look again at the life of Abraham. We saw in our previous lesson that God appeared to Abraham in a cloud of glory when Abraham was 75 years old. The Lord told him to leave his father's house and his country and journey to the geographic place that the Lord would reveal. Abraham accepted God's call and began his journey with Him.

Twenty-four years later, when Abraham was 99 years old, God appeared to him once again. Genesis 17:1 says:

> **And when Abram was ninety years old and nine, the Lord appeared to Abram, and said unto him, I am the Almighty God; walk before me, and be thou perfect.**

If you read this verse in Hebrew, it would make you laugh because God basically says, "…I am God Almighty; walk before me and stop messing up. Do exactly what I tell you to do."

Prior to this moment, Abraham had made a great many mistakes in his walk of faith, and at the age of 99, God spoke very plainly with him. Abraham heard the Lord, and from then on, he became more serious about being obedient in his life.

God went on to say in Genesis 17:2 and 3:

> **And I will make my covenant between me and thee, and will multiply thee exceedingly. And Abram fell on his face….**

Keep in mind, Abraham was 99 years old when God was telling him, "I'm going to multiply you exceedingly…." Realizing how old he is, Abraham fell on his face, probably overwhelmed and possibly in disbelief. The Lord continued to speak:

> **As for me, behold, my covenant is with thee, and thou shalt be a father of many nations. Neither shall thy name any more be called Abram, but thy name shall be Abraham; for a father of many nations have I made thee. And I will make thee exceeding**

fruitful, and I will make nations of thee, and kings shall come out of thee.

— Genesis 17:4-6

In these verses, we see that the Lord expanded His promise to Abram, telling him he would become the father of many nations and that kings would be produced through his lineage. Again, God was saying this to a man who was 99 years of age and had only one son at the time.

This encounter was so life-changing that the Lord changed Abram's name to Abraham, which means "father of many nations."

God Spoke to Abraham About Becoming a Father

During this same supernatural encounter, God shifted His attention to Abraham's wife Sarah, who, at the time, was named Sarai. The Bible says:

And God said unto Abraham, As for Sarai thy wife, thou shalt not call her name Sarai, but Sarah shall her name be. And I will bless her, and give thee a son also of her: yea, I will bless her, and she shall be a mother of nations; kings of people shall be of her.

— Genesis 17:15,16

Notice God said, "And I will *bless* her…." This is a power-drenched statement because when God speaks a *blessing* over a person's life, it empowers him or her with the ability to prosper in ways he or she could not function previously.

In Sarah's case, God was going to bless her 90-year-old body and empower her to conceive and give birth to a son — something her body could not naturally do on its own. Likewise, if you are in your senior years, God will speak a blessing over your life and empower you to do what you could not do in the natural.

What was Abraham's response to what God is saying? The Bible says:

Then Abraham fell upon his face, and laughed, and said in his heart, Shall a child be born unto him that is an hundred years old? and shall Sarah, that is ninety years old, bear?

— Genesis 17:17

Once more, Abraham fell to the ground — and this time he busted out laughing. In his mind, the idea of a 90-year-old woman and a nearly hundred-year-old man having a child was so impossible it was hilarious, and all he could do was laugh.

When Abraham finally gathered himself, he told God, "…O that Ishmael might live before thee!" (Genesis 17:18). Immediately, God responded and made His intentions crystal clear:

> …Sarah thy wife shall bear thee a son indeed; and thou shalt call his name Isaac: and I will establish my covenant with him for an everlasting covenant, and with his seed after him.
> — Genesis 17:19

God's plan would be fulfilled. A child would be born from the union of Abraham and Sarah — an act so impossible only God could get the credit for it. And the child's name was to be "Isaac," which means *laughter*. It is as if God was telling Abraham, "I see you're laughing at what I'm saying I'm going to do. So go ahead and name the child *laughter*, and we'll see who gets the last laugh."

After promising to take good care of Ishmael, God went on to say, "But my covenant will I establish with Isaac, which Sarah shall bear unto thee at this set time in the next year. And he left off talking with him, and God went up from Abraham" (Genesis 17:21,22).

Sarah Laughed at God's Promise

Shortly afterward, the Lord appeared once again to Abraham, and this time He came with two angels. Moved by the Lord's sudden and unexpected appearance, Abraham quickly made preparations for a meal to be served to his guests. As the Lord and the angels ate, the Lord asked Abraham:

> …Where is Sarah thy wife? And he said, Behold, in the tent. And he said, I will certainly return unto thee according to the time of life; and, lo, Sarah thy wife shall have a son. And Sarah heard it in the tent door, which was behind him. Now Abraham and Sarah were old and well stricken in age; and it ceased to be with Sarah after the manner of women.
> — Genesis 18:9-11

When the Lord told Abraham (a second time) that Sarah was going to have a baby, she overheard Him and began to laugh. The idea of her, a 90-year-old-woman, conceiving and giving birth to a child was hysterical.

When the Bible says, "Now Abraham and Sarah were old and well stricken in age; and it ceased to be with Sarah after the manner of women," it means in addition to them both being quite old, Sarah was *sterile* and well beyond the natural childbearing stage in a woman's life.

When Sarah heard the word of the Lord, she said:

> **Therefore Sarah laughed within herself, saying, After I am waxed old shall I have pleasure, my lord being old also?**
>
> **— Genesis 18:12**

If you read between the lines here, what Sarah is really saying is, "You've got to be kidding! Abraham and I are going to resume sexual activity? Do you not realize how old I am and how old he is?"

> **And the Lord said unto Abraham, Wherefore did Sarah laugh, saying, Shall I of a surety bear a child, which am old? Is any thing too hard for the Lord…?**
>
> **— Genesis 18:13,14**

Like Sarah and Abraham, what God has promised you may also seem impossible because of your age. But it doesn't matter how old you are, because nothing is too hard for the Lord. If God has made a promise to you, He intends to keep it. So don't give up on what He has told you He wants to do in your life. There's nothing too hard for the Lord! Your best years are in front of you, not behind you.

The Lord went on to say:

> **…At the time appointed I will return unto thee, according to the time of life, and Sarah shall have a son. Then Sarah denied, saying, I laughed not; for she was afraid. And he said, Nay; but thou didst laugh.**
>
> **— Genesis 18:14,15**

God's Promise Came To Pass!

When we read Genesis 21, we see God make good on His promise to both Abraham and Sarah. The Bible says, "And the Lord visited Sarah as he had said, and the Lord did unto Sarah as he had spoken" (Genesis 21:1). When it says the Lord "visited Sarah" and "did unto Sarah as he had spoken," it means God miraculously gave her the ability to receive seed and conceive a baby.

Scripture goes on to say:

> **For Sarah conceived, and bare Abraham a son in his old age, at the set time of which God had spoken to him. And Abraham called the name of his son that was born unto him, whom Sarah bare to him, Isaac. And Abraham circumcised his son Isaac being eight days old, as God had commanded him. And Abraham was an hundred years old, when his son Isaac was born unto him. And Sarah said, God hath made me to laugh, so that all that hear will laugh with me. And she said, Who would have said unto Abraham, that Sarah should have given children suck? for I have born him a son in his old age.**
> **— Genesis 21:2-7**

Can you imagine being 90 years old and having your first child? That was Sarah's story, and everyone who heard her testimony laughed with joy right along with her. As preposterous and outlandish the idea of having a baby at 90 years old was, it most certainly came to pass — just as the Lord had said. Sure enough, Sarah delivered Isaac and then nursed him in her arms in her old age. For with God, all things are possible! (See Matthew 19:26.)

The Book of Hebrews Documents Sarah's Faith and the Birth of Her Miracle

What is interesting about this story is that Sarah — like Abraham — is also mentioned in the Hebrews "Hall of Faith" chapter. And in this New Testament reference, we find some details about her life that we cannot find anywhere else. The Bible says:

> **Through faith also Sara herself received strength to conceive seed, and was delivered of a child when she was past age, because she judged him faithful who had promised.**
> **— Hebrews 11:11**

Sarah operated in faith and took ownership of God's strength.

Upon reading the opening words of this verse, we see that Sarah was using her faith. It wasn't just Abraham who was believing for the promise of God — Sarah was believing for it too. When we read this passage in the Greek, it actually begins by saying, "Through faith also Sara [being barren] herself…." The phrase says, "being barren" is derived from the Greek word *steiros*, which means *barren; sterile*; or *unable to produce children*.

The use of this word is what makes what happened so miraculous. Although Sarah was sterile and past the age of childrearing, she "received strength to conceive seed…." The word "received" here is taken from the word *lambano*, which means *to receive into one's possession* or *to take into one's own control and ownership*. It carries the idea of taking hold of something, grasping onto something, and embracing it so tightly that it becomes your very own.

The use of this word *lambano* reiterates the fact that Sarah had to actively engage her faith to receive God's strength. What He offered, she had to take ownership of and receive it as her personal possession. She had received a word from God that she would give birth to a son, but she had to believe that word and stand by it until the promise manifested in her life.

Again, the Scripture says she received "strength," which is the amazing Greek word *dunamis*, the word for *power*. It carries the idea of *explosive, superhuman power that comes with enormous energy and produces phenomenal, extraordinary, and unparalleled results*. With that power, her body was able to "conceive seed."

Sarah believed she would conceive when she was past the age of child-bearing.

In Greek, the word "conceive" is a translation of *katabole*, a compound of the word *kata*, meaning *down*, and *ballo*, meaning *to throw*. When compounded to form *katabole*, it describes *something being hurled down or forcibly put in place*. And the word "seed" is the Greek term *sperma*, which means *seed* or *sperm*.

The use of the words *katabole* (conceive) and *sperma* (seed) means that at age 90, Sarah was using her faith to believe for Abraham's seed to fertilize the egg in her womb as they came together in sexual intimacy at the ages of 99 and 90. And according to Hebrews 11:11, all of this occurred "…when she was past age…" (Hebrews 11:11).

This phrase "when she was past age" is a translation of the Greek words *kai para kairon helikias*, and it means *even well beyond a suitable age* or *beyond the years of opportunity*. In the natural, it was physically impossible for Sarah to conceive and give birth to a baby. But she had a word from God, and she held on to that word like a bulldog clutching its bone.

Sarah considered God to be absolutely faithful to keep His word.

When Sarah was well beyond the suitable age to conceive a child, "…she judged him faithful who had promised" (Hebrews 11:11). The Greek word for "judged" here is *hegeomai*, which means *to deem* or *to consider*, and the word "faithful" is the Greek word *piston*, meaning *absolutely faithful* or *absolutely trustworthy*.

Thus, when Sarah was well beyond the years of opportunity to bear a child, she considered God — "who had promised" — to be absolutely faithful and trustworthy. The words "who had promised" in Greek depict *one declaring and promising* or *the declarer and promiser*. Sarah took her eyes off of herself and the limitations of her old, feeble body, and she put them on God. She considered Him to be absolutely faithful and absolutely trustworthy to do what He promised.

God turned Abraham's sterility into *virility*.

Sarah took personal ownership of God's power by faith and believed He would take Abraham's seed and enable it to hit the target in her womb. The Bible says, "Therefore sprang there even of one, and him as good as dead, so many as the stars of the sky in multitude, and as the sand which is by the sea shore innumerable" (Hebrews 11:12).

Notice the phrase "as good as dead." It is translated from the Greek word *nenekromenou*, a compound of the words *nekroo*, meaning *lifeless; dead as a corpse; inoperative*; or *dead*. It refers to Abraham also being *sterile* before God quickened him.

Both he and Sarah had to be supernaturally renewed by the power of God, and once they were, out of them sprang as many children as the stars of the sky and the sand by the seashore. All of this happened to a woman who was 90 years old and a man who was 99 years old. Sarah gave birth to a baby, and both she and Abraham saw the plan of God come to pass for their life.

Friend, if you're in your senior years, it is time for you to get into agreement with God. It's not too late! God is ready to quicken you to do what is naturally impossible. Take His power by faith, and say, "I *will* give birth to the promise of God in my life, even if I'm in my older years. Although it may seem laughable and impossible, I believe these really are going to be the very best, most fruit-producing years of my life!"

STUDY QUESTIONS

Study to shew thyself approved unto God, a workman that needeth not to be ashamed, rightly dividing the word of truth.
— 2 Timothy 2:15

1. If God has made a promise to you, He will keep it. To help you stay in your place of faith and not give up hope for what He has told you, look up these powerful promises, jot them down in a Bible version that encourages you most, and commit them to memory.

    - **For God, nothing is impossible** — Genesis 18:14; Matthew 19:26; Luke 1:37

    - **He is Faithful** — Numbers 23:19; 1 Kings 8:56; Hebrews 6:18

    - **He is more than able** — Romans 16:25; Ephesians 3:20; Jude 24

2. Sarah took her eyes off of herself and the limitations of her old, feeble body, and she put them on God. She considered Him to be absolutely faithful and trustworthy to do what He promised. That's exactly what He wants *you* to do! So take time to reflect on these instructions to you:

    Keep your eyes on Jesus, who both began and finished this race we're in. Study how he did it. Because he never lost sight of where he was headed — that exhilarating finish in and with God — he could put up with anything along the way: Cross, shame, whatever. And now he's there, in the place of honor, right alongside God. When you find yourselves flagging in your faith, go over that story again, item by item, that long litany of hostility he plowed through. That will shoot adrenaline into your souls!
    — Hebrews 12:2,3 (*MSG*)

PRACTICAL APPLICATION

**But be ye doers of the word, and not hearers only,
deceiving your own selves.
— James 1:22**

1. The Bible says that God *blessed* Sarah in such a powerful way that her 90-year-old body was able to conceive and birth a child. Take a few moments to look back at your life. Describe some of the ways you know God has *blessed* you — moving in your life in such a miraculous way that you were able to do something you could not do previously.

2. Has God whispered a promise to you that seems so impossible that it is laughable? If so, briefly share what you believe He has spoken to you, and if you can remember, jot down how old you were when He first spoke it, as well as the details of any subsequent time the Holy Spirit reiterated this same word.

3. Read Matthew 7:7-11 and Romans 8:32. In what specific ways do you need God to bless you, your marriage, your family, your finances, or even your physical body so that you can experience the supernatural manifestation of what He has promised you? Begin to pray and ask the Holy Spirit to move in your life in this way — and *keep asking, seeking*, and *knocking* until what God promised comes to pass.

LESSON 6

TOPIC

Moses — Launching Out at 80 Years of Age

SCRIPTURES

1. **Hebrews 11:23** — By faith Moses, when he was born, was hid three months of his parents, because they saw he was a proper child....

2. **Acts 7:20** — In which time Moses was born, and was exceeding fair, and nourished up in his father's house three months.

3. **Hebrews 11:24** — By faith Moses, when he was come to years, refused to be called the son of Pharaoh's daughter.

4. **Acts 7:22** — And Moses was learned in all the wisdom of the Egyptians, and was mighty in words and in deeds.

5. **Hebrews 11:25-27** — Choosing rather to suffer affliction with the people of God, than to enjoy the pleasures of sin for a season; esteeming the reproach of Christ greater riches than the treasures in Egypt: for he had respect unto the recompence of the reward. By faith he forsook Egypt, not fearing the wrath of the king: for he endured, as seeing him who is invisible.

6. **Exodus 3:1-10** — Now Moses kept the flock of Jethro his father in law, the priest of Midian: and he led the flock to the backside of the desert, and came to the mountain of God, even to Horeb. And the angel of the Lord appeared unto him in a flame of fire out of the midst of a bush: and he looked, and, behold, the bush burned with fire, and the bush was not consumed. And Moses said, I will now turn aside, and see this great sight, why the bush is not burnt. And when the Lord saw that he turned aside to see, God called unto him out of the midst of the bush, and said, Moses, Moses. And he said, Here am I. And he said, Draw not nigh hither: put off thy shoes from off thy feet, for the place whereon thou standest is holy ground. Moreover he said, I am the God of thy father, the God of Abraham, the God of Isaac, and the God of Jacob. And Moses hid his face; for he was afraid to look upon God. And the Lord said, I have surely seen the affliction of my people which are in Egypt, and have heard their cry by reason of their taskmasters; for I know their sorrows; And I am come down to deliver them out of the hand of the Egyptians, and to bring them up out of that land unto a good land and a large, unto a land flowing with milk and honey; unto the place of the Canaanites, and the Hittites, and the Amorites, and the Perizzites, and the Hivites, and the Jebusites. Now therefore, behold, the cry of the children of Israel is come unto me: and I have also seen the oppression wherewith the Egyptians oppress them. Come now therefore, and I will send thee unto Pharaoh, that thou mayest bring forth my people the children of Israel out of Egypt.

7. **Exodus 4:10-12** — And Moses said unto the Lord, O my Lord, I am not eloquent, neither heretofore, nor since thou hast spoken unto thy servant: but I am slow of speech, and of a slow tongue. And the Lord said unto him, Who hath made man's mouth? or who maketh the dumb, or deaf, or the seeing, or the blind? have not I the Lord? Now

therefore go, and I will be with thy mouth, and teach thee what thou shalt say

8. **Deuteronomy 34:7** — And Moses was an hundred and twenty years old when he died: his eye was not dim, nor his natural force abated.

GREEK WORDS

1. "proper child" — **ἀστεῖος** (*asteios*): polished; elegant; sophisticated; unusual

2. "exceeding fair" — **ἀστεῖος** (*asteios*): polished; elegant; sophisticated; unusual

3. "come to years" — **γενόμενος μέγας** (*genomenos megas*): literally, having become great

4. "learned" — **παιδεύω** (*paideuo*): to nourish; to fully educate and instruct; to educate from childhood to adulthood refers to both natural and religious education

5. "all" — **πάσῃ** (*pase*): an all-encompassing term meaning all, with nothing excluded

6. "wisdom" — **σοφία** (*sophia*): insight, skill, intelligence, philosophy, sophistication; especially astute, bright, educated, smart, or eminently enlightened

7. "mighty" — **δυνατὸς** (*dunatos*): a powerful force; amazing ability; to be able, capable, or competent for any task; a force that causes one to be able or capable; one who is competent; often refers to people who have political power or political might; the idea of one who is mighty in the world's view

8. "refused" — **ἀρνέομαι** (*arneomai*): to deny, to disown, to reject, to refuse, or to renounce; referred to a person who disavowed, forsook, walked away from, or washed one's hands of another person or group of people; such denials were usually accompanied with ridicule or persecution

9. "choosing" — **ἱρέω** (*haireo*): to choose or prefer; depicts a personal choice or preference that sets one apart from others

10. "suffer affliction with" — **συγκακουχέω** (*sunkakoucheo*): depicts joint suffering; to suffer bad things in partnership with others

11. "esteeming" — **ἡγέομαι** (*hegeomai*): to count; to deem; to consider

12. "reproach" — **ονειδισμός** (*oneidismos*): insults; pictures language intended to injure, harm, hurt, or damage; denotes words that damage one's reputation

13. "riches" — **πλούσιος** (*plousios*): wealth so great it cannot be tabulated; abundant or vast wealth; extreme riches; unlimited wealth; incredible abundance; opulence; or extravagant lavishness; pictures someone who possesses incredible abundance, extreme wealth, and enormous affluence

14. "forsook" — **καταλείπω** (*kataleipo*): to abandon and leave behind

15. "wrath" — **θυμός** (*thumos*): portrays a person who suddenly flares up and loses control; one who boils with anger and blows up, erupting in an ugly outburst that negatively affects other people

16. "endured" — **καρτερέω** (*kartereo*): to continue undeterred; to be steadfast; to persevere; to stay on track

SYNOPSIS

In our first five lessons, we discovered that God wants to bless each of us with longevity and empower us to be highly productive all the way to the end of our life. We also examined the lives of several individuals who lived long and were extremely fruitful.

First, we looked at Enoch who experienced the greatest move of God in his life when he was 365 years old. Then we learned about Noah who had a spiritual awakening at age 500 and was given the assignment to build an ark for the saving of his family and the preservation of the world.

Next, we examined the life of Abraham and saw how God called him at the age of 75, and then appeared to him again at age 99. Abraham was then given a prophetic word from the Lord that he and his wife, Sarah, were going to have a baby, and sure enough, within less than a year, Sarah delivered a baby boy, and they named him Isaac.

In each of these situations, God did what was impossible in the natural, proving that nothing is too difficult for Him. Indeed, the senior years of our life are designed to be the most marvelous and productive of all. What God did in these people's lives He longs to do in yours!

The emphasis of this lesson:

From the time Moses was three months old to age 40, Moses was raised and educated in the wisdom and ways of the Egyptians, but at age 40, he was awakened to his Hebrew family ties. For the next 40 years, God prepared him in the wilderness, and at age 80 he encountered God like never before, receiving a brand-new assignment and being catapulted into the greatest season of his life.

Your Best Is Yet To Come!

As we have noted in our previous lessons, while many individuals between the ages of 50 and 60 are thinking about retirement, they are actually just on the brink of the most productive decades of their life. Current statistics regarding our latter years indicate that…

- The most productive age is from 60 to 70 years of age.
- The second most productive stage is from 70 to 80 years of age.
- The third most productive stage is from 50 to 60 years of age.

Without question, our senior years are truly designed to be the golden years of our life. Consider these facts:

- The average age of Nobel Prize winners is late 60s and early 70s.
- The average age of presidents of large companies is 57 to 60 years.
- The average age of pastors of the 100 largest churches in the U.S. is 71 years.
- The average age of individuals who become Popes is 78 years.

All these studies taken together reveal that the best years of your life are between the ages of 60 and 80. At 60 years of age, you begin to reach your potential, and this continues into your 80s. If you're between the ages of 60 and 70, you're in the best mental level of your life. And if you are between the ages of 70 and 80, you are in the second-best mental level of your life.

Someone might say, "If my best mental years are between ages 60 and 80, why do I seem to be losing my memory?" Well, these same studies on the high productivity of our golden years also show that what many people deem to be memory loss is actually *mental overload*. In other words, people's minds are so filled with information that they experience a strain on their brain so intense, their thinking begins to short-circuit in some ways, which makes sense because, as we get older, our base of knowledge and experience increases substantially.

Moreover, by the time you reach 60 years of age, you are able to think faster and make decisions quicker because you've learned many hard lessons in life. Now you are ready to really thrive in your senior years.

If you think about it, in your first 30 years of life, you're learning. In your second 30 years, you are working and doing. And in your third 30 years, you should be helping, imparting to, and investing time into others.

It is a grave mistake to move off the playing field and head to the locker room simply because you're older. For example, if you're a pastor in your early 60s and you're thinking about retiring, please think again. Although it is wonderful to bring the younger generation into areas of leadership, your age does not lessen the value of your contribution. On the contrary! It would be a huge loss to the congregation and the community you're serving if you sell yourself short. Your age should never stop you from serving God and pursuing His call on your life. Again, your best years are still in front of you!

Moses Was an Extraordinary Child

From the death of Abraham to the birth of Moses is about 250 years. Clearly, Moses was a man God used mightily to deliver the people of Israel from Egyptian slavery and establish them as a nation. Moses' story is included in both the Old and New Testaments, and like Abraham and Sarah, he is also included in the legendary "Hall of Faith" chapter of Hebrews.

By faith Moses, when he was born, was hid three months of his parents, because they saw he was a proper child....
— Hebrews 11:23

The words "proper child" are a translation of the Greek word *asteios*, which is from where we get the English word *aesthetics*, and it describes some-thing *polished*; *elegant*; *sophisticated*; or *unusual*. When Moses' parents saw him, they knew there was something special and unusual about him. This idea is reiterated by Stephen in Acts 7:20, where he says:

In which time Moses was born, and was exceeding fair, and nourished up in his father's house three months.

That phrase "exceeding fair" is the same Greek word *asteios*. Again, it means to be *polished, elegant, sophisticated,* or *unusual.* From the moment of his birth, Moses' mom and dad knew he was a remarkable child — even aesthetically. There was just something about him that was visually appealing.

At the time of Moses' birth, Pharaoh, the head of all Egypt, had commanded that every Hebrew male child born was to be killed (*see* Exodus 1:15,16). Specifically, he said they were to be thrown into the river and drowned (*see* Exodus 1:22). But Moses' parents loved him and saw that there was something extraordinary about him, so they hid him and took good care of him for three months.

Exodus 2:3 says, "And when she could not longer hide him, she took for him an ark of bulrushes, and daubed it with slime and with pitch, and put the child therein; and she laid it in the flags by the river's brink" (Exodus 2:3). Once Moses was in the woven basket of bulrushes and placed on the water, it floated to where the daughter of Pharaoh came to the river to bathe. She found Moses and took him into her home and raised him as her own.

Moses Was Educated and Trained in Every Aspect of Egyptian Wisdom

From the time Moses was three months old to age 40, Moses was raised as an Egyptian in the daughter of Pharoah's home. It wasn't until he was 40 years old that he had a revelation of who he really was and discovered his Hebrew roots. In the "Hall of Faith," the writer of Hebrews described this moment:

> **By faith Moses, when he was come to years, refused to be called the son of Pharaoh's daughter.**
> **— Hebrews 11:24**

The phrase "come to years" in the original Greek literally says, "Having become great." Thus, it doesn't refer so much to his age as to his *stature.* By the time Moses reached 40 years of age, he was *great in stature.* In fact, if you read the writings of Josephus, you will find he described in vivid detail Moses' stature in Egypt. Moses was very wise and had racked up many notable achievements before he identified with the people of God.

This fact is also mentioned by Stephen as he retold the highlights of Israeli history to the Jewish leaders:

And Moses was learned in all the wisdom of the Egyptians, and was mighty in words and in deeds.

— Acts 7:22

There are several words in this verse that are important to understand. The first is "learned," which is translated from the Greek word *paideuo*, and it means *to nourish*. It carries the idea of *fully educating and instructing from childhood to adulthood* and refers to both *natural and religious education*. Thus, in every respect, from the time Moses was three months old to age 40, Moses had been raised, nurtured, and educated as an Egyptian.

This brings us to the word "all" — the Greek word *pase* — which is an all-encompassing term meaning *all, with nothing excluded*. The word "wisdom" in Greek is *sophia*, which describes *insight, skill, intelligence, philosophy*, and *sophistication*. The use of the word *sophia* means Moses was especially *astute, bright, educated, smart*, and *eminently enlightened*.

According to Acts 7:22, in addition to being schooled in the very best Egypt had to offer, Moses was also "…mighty in words and in deeds." The word "mighty" here is the Greek word *dunatos*, which describes *a powerful force* and *amazing ability*. It means *to be able, capable*, or *competent for any task*. It is *a force that causes one to be able or capable* and can also be translated as *one who is competent*.

Often, this word *dunatos* refers to people who have political power or political might. It is the idea of one who is mighty in the world's view. Specifically, the Scripture says Moses was mighty "in words," which means *in speech* and *in vocabulary*, and in "deeds," which describes *actions, deeds*, or *works*. This gives us a detailed description of Moses' great status at age 40.

Moses Renounced His Egyptian Status and Chose To Suffer Affliction With God's People

Yet, despite the greatness achieved by Moses in the world's eyes, according to Hebrews 11:24, "…[he] refused to be called the son of Pharaoh's daughter." In Greek, the word "refused" is *arneomai*, and it means *to deny, to disown, to reject, to refuse*, or *to renounce*. It referred to *a person who disavowed, forsook, walked away from*, or *washed one's hands of another person or group of people*, and such denials were usually accompanied with ridicule or persecution.

So when Moses renounced that he was the son of Pharaoh's daughter and refused the rank of being an Egyptian prince, he dealt with a great deal of ridicule and persecution. Why did Moses wash his hands and walk away from his high-ranking status as an Egyptian? The Bible says:

> **Choosing rather to suffer affliction with the people of God, than to enjoy the pleasures of sin for a season.**
> — **Hebrews 11:25**

Notice the word "choosing." It is a form of the Greek word *haireo*, which means *to choose or prefer*. It depicts *a personal choice or preference that sets one apart from others*. Although it was unthinkable in the eyes of the Egyptians for Moses to prefer "suffering affliction with the people of God," that is exactly what he chose. And the phrase "suffer affliction with" in Greek depicts *joint suffering* or *to suffer bad things in partnership with others*.

Moses saw the affliction that the Hebrew people were suffering and chose to suffer with them himself rather than "...to enjoy the pleasures of sin for a season" (Hebrews 11:25). The word "enjoy" here is *apolausis* in Greek, and it describes *enjoyment* or *benefits*. Moses rejected the pleasures of sin, which only last for a "season," and in the original Greek means *a limited season* or *for a temporary season*.

The 'Reproach of Christ'
Yields Far Greater Riches

Instead of lavishing himself in the best of what the world had to offer, Moses walked away from it all...

> **Esteeming the reproach of Christ greater riches than the treasures in Egypt: for he had respect unto the recompence of the reward.**
> — **Hebrew 11:26**

The opening word "esteeming" is translated from the Greek word *hegeomai*, which means *to count*; *to deem*; or *to consider*. The use of *hegeomai* tells us that Moses really put his mind to thinking through and calculating the decision he needed to make. In the end, he counted "...the reproach of Christ greater riches than the treasures of Egypt" (Hebrews 11:26).

In Greek, the word "reproach" is *oneidismos*, and it describes *insults*. It pictures *language intended to injure, harm, hurt,* or *damage*, and it denotes *words that damage one's reputation*. This tells us that when Moses walked away from the lap of luxury in Egypt and chose to identify with the people of God, he subjected himself to a great deal of verbal abuse.

Of course, when we think about Egypt, we often think about "treasures," which in this verse is the word *thesauros*, and it describes *treasure; a treasury; a treasure chamber*, or *a place of safekeeping where riches and fortunes are kept*. It describes Egypt's massive riches and wealth, Moses chose the reproach of Christ and called it *greater riches*.

The word "riches" is the fabulous Greek word *plousios*, and it describes *wealth so great it cannot be tabulated*. It is *abundant or vast wealth; extreme riches; unlimited wealth; incredible abundance; opulence*; or *extravagant lavishness*. This word *plousios* pictures someone who possesses incredible abundance, extreme wealth, and enormous affluence.

Amazingly, this is the word that was used to describe the way Moses viewed the insults and verbal abuse, or reproach, that came with following Christ. He saw that in Christ, there are abundant riches beyond anything he had ever seen in the treasures of Egypt. These same riches are available to all believers in Christ — including *you*.

Moses Abandoned Egypt and Endured Pharaoh's Wrath

Rather than revel in the lofty position of being called the son of Pharaoh's daughter or enjoy the temporary pleasures of sin or bask in the wealth and treasures of Egypt, "By faith he [Moses] forsook Egypt, not fearing the wrath of the king: for he endured, as seeing him who is invisible" (Hebrews 11:27).

The word "forsook" is the Greek word *kataleipo*, and it means *to abandon and leave behind*. Moses abandoned and left Egypt behind, "…not fearing the wrath of the king…" (Hebrews 11:27). In Greek, the word "wrath" is a form of the word *thumos*, and it portrays *a person who suddenly flares up and loses control* or *one who boils with anger and blows up, erupting in an ugly outburst that negatively affects other people*.

Moses knew Pharaoh (the king) was going to be angry and have outbursts of wrath over his walking away from his Egyptian identity, but he chose to *endure* that wrath. The Greek word for "endured" is *kartereo*, which means *to continue undeterred; to be steadfast; to persevere*; or *to stay on track*. Moses refused to let anything move him off course with his decision to follow God. All these things occurred when he was 40 years of age.

By his own choice, Moses abandoned everything he knew in Egypt and ended up out in the wilderness for his next 40 years of life. From the ages of 40 to 80, he wandered from one pasture to another, taking care of his father-in-law Jethro's sheep. It was during those 40 years of testing that God worked on Moses.

Although he may not have realized it, he was being emptied of all his pride, his previous identity, and his false ambition. All the natural skills he had previously leaned upon were taken away, until, finally, when he reached the age of 80, he was ready to be used by God. It was at that point that he had an encounter with the Almighty.

The Burning Bush Experience

What took place between Moses and God on Mount Horeb is written down in detail for us to read. Keep in mind that as you reflect on these verses, you are reading through the personal retelling of the one who experienced it. The Bible says:

Now Moses kept the flock of Jethro his father in law, the priest of Midian: and he led the flock to the backside of the desert, and came to the mountain of God, even to Horeb. And the angel of the LORD appeared unto him in a flame of fire out of the midst of a bush: and he looked, and, behold, the bush burned with fire, and the bush was not consumed. And Moses said, I will now turn aside, and see this great sight, why the bush is not burnt. And when the LORD saw that he turned aside to see, God called unto him out of the midst of the bush, and said, Moses, Moses. And he said, Here am I. And he said, Draw not nigh hither: put off thy shoes from off thy feet, for the place whereon thou standest is holy ground. Moreover he said, I am the God of thy father, the God of Abraham, the God of Isaac, and the God of Jacob. And Moses hid his face; for he was afraid to look upon God. And the LORD said, I have surely seen the affliction of my people which are in Egypt, and have heard their cry by reason of their taskmasters; for I know their sorrows; And I am come down to deliver them out of the hand of the Egyptians, and to bring them up out of that land unto a

good land and a large, unto a land flowing with milk and honey; unto the place of the Canaanites, and the Hittites, and the Amorites, and the Perizzites, and the Hivites, and the Jebusites. Now therefore, behold, the cry of the children of Israel is come unto me: and I have also seen the oppression wherewith the Egyptians oppress them. Come now therefore, and I will send thee unto Pharaoh, that thou mayest bring forth my people the children of Israel out of Egypt.

— Exodus 3:1-10

Moses was 80 years old when he encountered God in the burning bush. He was now in the golden years of his life, and he was primed and prepared to experience the greatest, most powerful season of usefulness to and intimacy with God.

God Qualified and Enabled Moses To Accomplish His Assignment

Ecclesiastes 3:1 (*NKJV*) says, "To everything there is a season, a time for every purpose under heaven." After Moses' burning bush encounter with God, he was not the same. Everything changed, and he entered a brand-new season of life.

Still, there were times when Moses struggled to accept and walk in obedience to God, just like we do at times. After God instructed him to return to Pharaoh and demand that the Hebrew people be set free, "…Moses said unto the Lord, O my Lord, I am not eloquent, neither heretofore, nor since thou hast spoken unto thy servant: but I am slow of speech, and of a slow tongue" (Exodus 4:10).

What is interesting and amusing about this passage is that earlier in Moses' life, he was known to be "mighty in words" (*see* Acts 7:22). However, after 40 years of wandering in the wilderness and spending most of his time with sheep, Moses had lost his eloquence, and he knew it. To this, the Lord answered him and said:

…Who hath made man's mouth? or who maketh the dumb, or deaf, or the seeing, or the blind? have not I the Lord? Now therefore go, and I will be with thy mouth, and teach thee what thou shalt say

— Exodus 4:11,12

This rebuttal from God was the equivalent of Him saying, "Hey, Moses, I made your mouth and have given you the ability to speak. So even if you think you're not qualified or eloquent, I will qualify you and enable you to speak — even at age 80." Moses was about to enter the most fruitful years of his life — his senior years. Everything he had done and endured for the 80 years leading up to that moment was all in preparation for the primary role for his life — to deliver and lead the people of Israel and be God's lawgiver.

Unabated Strength and Health Are Promised to You by God

The Bible says that in the end, when Moses accomplished what God had called him to do, "…Moses was an hundred and twenty years old when he died: his eye was not dim, nor his natural force abated" (Deuteronomy 34:7).

Friend, that is what God wants for you! He wants you to press forward into your senior years with hope and faith to accomplish His plan for your life. If Moses could finish his race with unabated strength and health, so can you! Remember, God's desire is for you to go from strength to strength (*see* Psalm 84:7.) He wants you to go out in a blaze of His glory.

If you're entering your senior years, don't say, "I guess my best years are behind me." Instead, begin to say, "I believe my best days are *in front of me*, and my senior years will be my golden years! Father, I'm ready for a fresh encounter with You that will set me on a new trajectory. These will be the greatest fruit-producing years of my life!"

[For an in-depth look at the life of Moses, we recommend you obtain Rick's ten-part series entitled *Moses and the Ten Plagues*. You can order it at **renner.org** or by calling 1-800-742-5593.]

STUDY QUESTIONS

**Study to shew thyself approved unto God, a workman that needeth not to be ashamed, rightly dividing the word of truth.
— 2 Timothy 2:15**

1. There are many facts about Moses presented in this lesson. Which ones were new or intriguing to you? How do all these details help you see Moses in a different light?

2. Carefully read and compare Hebrews 11:24-27 and Philippians 2:5-8. What parallels between *Moses* and *Jesus* do you observe?
3. Read Matthew 5:10-12 and Romans 8:17. When Moses renounced his position as the son of Pharoah's daughter and refused the rank of being an Egyptian prince, he dealt with a great deal of ridicule and persecution. What does God promise us when we are ridiculed and persecuted for His sake?

PRACTICAL APPLICATION

But be ye doers of the word, and not hearers only,
deceiving your own selves.
— James 1:22

1. God worked on and prepared Moses in the wilderness for 40 years — emptying him of pride, selfish ambition, and his previous identity before launching him into his lifetime calling. In what areas can you now see that God has worked on, changed, and shaped you to be more like Jesus?
2. Read Second Corinthians 12:9 and 10. When the Lord commissioned Moses to deliver the people of Israel from bondage, Moses objected, saying he had lost his eloquence of speech. How about *you*? What perceived flaw or weakness causes you to feel disqualified from God's call? Bring your objections to Him in prayer, asking Him to qualify and enable you to accomplish what He is asking you to do.

LESSON 7

TOPIC

Caleb — Asking for a New Assignment at 85 Years of Age

SCRIPTURES

1. **Psalm 91:16** — With long life will I satisfy him, and shew him my salvation.

2. **Numbers 14:24** — But my servant Caleb, because he had another spirit with him, and hath followed me fully, him will I bring into the land whereinto he went; and his seed shall possess it.

3. **Joshua 14:7** — Forty years old was I when Moses the servant of the Lord sent me from Kadeshbarnea to espy out the land; and I brought him word again as it was in mine heart.

4. **Numbers 13:30** — And Caleb stilled the people before Moses, and said, Let us go up at once, and possess it; for we are well able to overcome it.

5. **Joshua 14:8-12** — Nevertheless my brethren that went up with me made the heart of the people melt: but I wholly followed the Lord my God. And Moses sware on that day, saying, Surely the land whereon thy feet have trodden shall be thine inheritance, and thy children's for ever, because thou hast wholly followed the Lord my God. And now, behold, the Lord hath kept me alive, as he said, these forty and five years, even since the Lord spake this word unto Moses, while the children of Israel wandered in the wilderness: and now, lo, I am this day fourscore and five years old. As yet I am as strong this day as I was in the day that Moses sent me: as my strength was then, even so is my strength now, for war, both to go out, and to come in. Now therefore give me this mountain, whereof the Lord spake in that day; for thou heardest in that day how the Anakims were there, and that the cities were great and fenced: if so be the Lord will be with me, then I shall be able to drive them out, as the Lord said.

SYNOPSIS

Is a brand-new encounter with God for someone in his or her senior years possible? Absolutely! **Enoch** reached the peak of his spiritual life and had a new encounter with God at age 365. It was at age 500 that **Noah** began hearing from God like never before and received his new assignment to preserve his family and a sampling of all life.

Abraham met the Lord in a magnificent way at age 75, which put him on a whole new trajectory. Then at age 99, God told him he was going to father a child with Sarah, his 90-year-old wife, who also received the same prophetic word and trusted God to make it happen.

Then there's **Moses**, a man who experienced a divine encounter with God at age 40, and the course of his life was redirected. For the next four decades, as he shepherded sheep and wandered in the wilderness, the Lord worked on him, emptying him of all the things he had picked up in Egypt, including pride, prestige, self-ambition, and self-importance. Finally, at age 80 he was ready to be used mightily of God.

If you've wondered if you have wasted a part of your life, it might be that God was getting you ready for what is just over the horizon. Moses was 80 years old when he encountered God on Mount Horeb, and that triggered the greatest season of his life. He lived until he was 120, and when he died, his eye was not dim, nor his strength abated (*see* Deuteronomy 34:7). *That is God's will for you!* He wants you to go from strength to strength (*see* Psalm 84:7). So, don't disqualify yourself just because you're a little older. Now, more than ever, you are finally ready for God's new assignment.

The emphasis of this lesson:

Caleb served God wholeheartedly, and the Bible says he was a man with "another spirit." His eyes were fixed on God's faithfulness, and he remained uncompromisingly devoted to the Lord, regardless of how much criticism and ridicule was brought against him. Caleb repeatedly gave God glory for all the good he accomplished, and he was just as strong at 85 as he was at 40.

A Quick Review of Our Anchor Verse

To anyone who "dwells in the secret place of the Most High" and "abides under the shadow of the Almighty," God promises great blessings! (*See* Psalm 91:1.) One of the greatest blessings is found in Psalm 91:16, where God declares:

With long life will I satisfy him, and shew him my salvation.

In this, our anchor verse, we have noted several important words, including the word "long." It is from a Hebrew word that speaks of *length of days*, and it implies *longevity*. The word "life" is the term for *days*. When these words are joined as the phrase "long life," it depicts *long days* or *a very long life*.

God says that with a very long life He will "satisfy" us, and that word "satisfy" means *to have enough*, *to have plenty of*, or *to be fully satisfied*. The fact that God wants us *to have enough* and *be fully satisfied* with the number of days we have on the earth means He doesn't want us to check out of this life prematurely.

In fact, throughout your life, He wants to show you His *salvation*. The word "salvation" in Hebrew includes *healing*, *wholeness*, and *soundness of mind*, which means you don't have to lose your memory or live with dementia when you get older. God wants to parade everything that's packed in His salvation into your life, all the way up to the end! Friend, that is God's promise to you, but in order to receive it, you must take it by faith.

Recent Studies on Aging Deviate From Traditional Thinking

When most people contemplate getting old, they think about their body and mind progressively losing ability and winding down. Surprisingly, what new studies on aging reveal flies in the face of traditional thinking. For example, recent statistics regarding our latter years of life indicate that…

- The most productive age is from 60 to 70 years.
- The second most productive stage is from 70 to 80 years of age.
- The third most productive stage is from 50 to 60 years of age.

So when most people are thinking about retirement and a life without work, they really should be focusing on making the most of the greatest season of their life that is right in front of them. At 60 years of age, we know what works and doesn't work, we know what's right and what's wrong, and we have enough knowledge and experience to really get things done. Maybe that is why…

- The average age of Nobel Prize winners is late 60s to early 70s.
- The average age of presidents of leading companies is 57 to 60 years.
- The average age of pastors of the 100 largest churches in the U.S. is 71 years.
- The average age of individuals who become Popes is 78 years.

Clearly, the best years of your life are between the ages of 60 and 80. At age 60, you begin to reach your potential, and this continues all the way into your 80s. Statistically, if you're between the ages of 60 and 70, you're in the best mental fitness of your life, and if you are between the ages of 70 and 80, you are in the second-best mental state of your life. So if you are anywhere between the ages of 60 and 80, you should begin to declare that you are in the *best* season of your life!

The truth is, during the first 30 years of life, you're *learning*. In the second 30 years of life, you are *working* and *doing*. And in the third 30 years, you should be investing time imparting to and helping others. Friend, God wants you to flourish in your senior years and be fully satisfied with the days He gives you.

Caleb Was a Man With 'Another Spirit'

Another biblical figure from the time of Moses who sometimes gets overlooked is Caleb. The Bible says Caleb descended from the tribe of Judah (*see* Numbers 13:6), and it seems that he was a godly man from the beginning. God Himself spoke to Moses about Caleb and said:

> **But my servant Caleb, because he had another spirit with him, and hath followed me fully, him will I bring into the land whereinto he went; and his seed shall possess it.**
> **— Numbers 14:24**

This was God's assessment of Caleb! He was different from the others in Israel in that he served God wholeheartedly and passionately. Like Joshua, Caleb had a different spirit from the other ten spies who went in to evaluate the Promised Land.

Caleb Was Focused on God's Faithfulness

The Bible says ten of the twelve spies who explored the new territory came back saying, "…The people be strong that dwell in the land, and the cities are walled, and very great: and moreover we saw the children of Anak there" (Numbers 13:28).

The children of Anak were *giants*, which is what the ten spies went on to say: "And there we saw the giants, the sons of Anak, which come of the giants: and we were in our own sight as grasshoppers, and so we were in their sight" (Numbers 13:33).

Although the ten spies did acknowledge that the land was beautiful and filled with amazing fruit and fertile pastures, their focus stayed on the giants. As a result of their misplaced focus, the ten spies melted with fear and brought the people an "evil report."

The ten evil spies got exactly what they saw. Because they were fearful, faithless, and remained like grasshoppers in their own sight, they did not enter the Promised Land. On the other hand, Caleb and Joshua were of a different spirit. Although they didn't deny that there were giants in the land, they chose to fix their eyes on the magnificent fruit and the amazing God they served — *and they got what they saw.*

This sobering example should cause us to step back and evaluate our focus. What we see is what we will receive. So we must be sure our eyes are fixed on God and what He has said belongs to us. We must not focus on the negative hindrances but on the unmatched power of God and His faithful track record to deliver what He has promised. This positive perspective will always produce positive results.

Caleb Was a Bold, Passionate Man of Conviction

In addition to being God-focused and bringing a good report, Caleb was also unabashedly bold about his devotion to God. When the time came for the Promised Land to be parceled out to the various tribes of Israel, Caleb spoke up and told Joshua:

> **Forty years old was I when Moses the servant of the Lord sent me from Kadeshbarnea to spy out the land; and I brought him word again as it was in mine heart.**
>
> **— Joshua 14:7**

Isn't that interesting? Like Moses, Caleb was also selected when he was 40 years old. It seems that the age of 40 is a pivotal year for many people to hear from God and receive a specific assignment for their life. Caleb stayed on track his whole life, and his obedience to God shaped the next 45 years of his life.

Note the strong conviction in Caleb's voice. His convictions went against the grain of the ten negative spies, and regardless of how much criticism and ridicule was brought against him or how unpopular and out of step he was with the others, he was not influenced by others' negativity.

To be clear, what the other ten spies saw was *accurate* — there really were giants in the new land. But these fearful leaders of Israel had completely left God out of the picture! They walked by sight — not faith — and consequently, they gave a message of doom and gloom that was so infectious that the people's hearts were melted with fear.

Unlike the others, Caleb was not moved by fear. As the ten faithless spies were voicing their evil report to the people, "…Caleb stilled the people before Moses, and said, Let us go up at once, and possess it; for we are well able to overcome it" (Numbers 13:30).

Again, we hear the strong conviction in Caleb's voice. He had a personal revelation of God and knew who he was with God on his side. Even though the odds of defeating the giants seemed insurmountable, Caleb believed the impossible was possible through the power of God! Through his fearless, bold faith, he was ready to tackle an impossible assignment — even at age 40.

Caleb Was Always Careful To Give God the Glory

Returning to the post-battle settlement of the land, Caleb was now 85 years old, and he was just as bold and confident in his senior years as he was at age 40. As he retold the account of the twelve spies who went in to survey the land, he said to Joshua:

> **Nevertheless my brethren that went up with me made the heart of the people melt: but I wholly followed the Lord my God. And Moses sware on that day, saying, Surely the land whereon thy feet have trodden shall be thine inheritance, and thy children's forever, because thou hast wholly followed the Lord my God.**
>
> **— Joshua 14:8,9**

In this passage, we see that Caleb unashamedly declared his undivided, deep devotion to the Lord. This is one of six passages in Scripture where Caleb is described as a man who served God wholeheartedly! He was passionate about serving God, and he sought to do so with all his heart, soul, mind, and strength.

As Caleb continued talking to Joshua and rehearsing what happened more than 45 years earlier, he went on to say:

> **And now, behold, the Lord hath kept me alive, as he said, these forty and five years, even since the Lord spake this word unto**

Moses, while the children of Israel wandered in the wilderness: and now, lo, I am this day fourscore and five years old.

— Joshua 14:10

Here, Caleb acknowledged that it was God who had kept him alive and had given him the strength to persevere through all of Israel's wanderings in the wilderness. For 45 years, Caleb maintained a consistent walk of faith. Despite the faithlessness of the ten spies and the rebellious ways of the children of Israel, he remained on track with God.

Caleb went on to say:

As yet I am as strong this day as I was in the day that Moses sent me: as my strength was then, even so is my strength now, for war, both to go out, and to come in.

— Joshua 14:11

Keep in mind, Caleb was 85 years old when he spoke these words. Without hesitation, he declared that he was just as strong at 85 as he was at age 40 when Moses initially sent him out to survey the land with the other spies. Amazingly, at 85 years of age Caleb was ready for anything — even to go out to war if necessary.

Caleb Was Ready for a New Assignment Even in His Senior Years

Rather than just sitting, relaxing, and riding out the remainder of his years taking it easy, Caleb was ready and eager for a new assignment, which is why he said:

Now therefore give me this mountain, whereof the Lord spake in that day; for thou heardest in that day how the Anakims were there, and that the cities were great and fenced: if so be the Lord will be with me, then I shall be able to drive them out, as the Lord said.

— Joshua 14:12

The Anakims that Caleb spoke of here were considered to be the biggest and most fierce of all the giants. Amazingly, when other men's hearts were trembling for fear, Caleb had such a strong conviction of the unmatched power of the Spirit of God working through him that he was ready to take on and defeat another round of giants to have what the Lord had promised.

In modern-day language, it is as if Caleb was saying: "I might be 85 years old, but I want a new assignment. Give me that mountain — the big one filled with the biggest, most ferocious giants of all, where the cities are fenced up to the heavens. That's the one I want. And the Lord will be with me, and we will drive them out!"

Friend, if you are in your senior years, know that it is God's will for you to be mighty and to flourish. Like Caleb, you can boldly pray, "Lord, with all the experience I have behind me and the faithfulness You've proven to me throughout my life, I'm ready for a new, big assignment!"

STUDY QUESTIONS

**Study to shew thyself approved unto God, a workman that needeth not to be ashamed, rightly dividing the word of truth.
— 2 Timothy 2:15**

1. Caleb was passionate about serving God, and he sought to do so with all his heart, soul, mind, and strength. Read Matthew 22:37 and 38 and Mark 12:29 and 30. According to Jesus' words, what does Caleb's life exemplify?

2. Caleb had a personal revelation that God was all-powerful, and He was on his side. To help you really know that God has your back and is on your side, take some time to meditate on these powerful promises:

What then shall we say to [all] this? If God is for us, who [can be] against us? [Who can be our foe, if God is on our side?] He who did not withhold or spare [even] His own Son but gave Him up for us all, will He not also with Him freely and graciously give us all [other] things?
— Romans 8:31,32 (*AMPC*)

The Lord God is my Strength, my personal bravery, and my invincible army; He makes my feet like hinds' feet and will make me to walk [not to stand still in terror, but to walk] and make [spiritual] progress upon my high places [of trouble, suffering, or responsibility]!
— Habakkuk 3:19 (*AMPC*)

'I [Jesus] give them real and eternal life. They are protected
from the Destroyer for good. No one can steal them from out
of my hand. The Father who put them under my care is so much
greater than the Destroyer and Thief. No one could ever get
them away from him. I and the Father are one heart and mind.'
— John 10:28-30 (*MSG*)

PRACTICAL APPLICATION

But be ye doers of the word, and not hearers only,
deceiving your own selves.
— James 1:22

1. The ten spies who brought an evil report did acknowledge that the
   land was beautiful and filled with amazing fruit. However, they
   focused their attention on the giants, and as a result, they melted
   with fear. Be honest with yourself: Where is your focus? Is it on your
   "giant" problems or on the greatness of God? What kind of fruit is
   being produced in your life as a result?

2. The Bible instructs us to "remember the deeds of the Lord" and to
   "meditate on all His mighty works" (*see* Psalm 77:11,12). Look back
   over your life and recall the times God showed up and *provided* for
   you, *protected* you, *promoted* you, and *forgave* you. Rather than focus
   on the hindrances at hand, focus on the faithfulness of your Heavenly
   Father, and magnify Him with your praise! He was faithful to deliver
   you before, and He will be faithful again!

LESSON 8

TOPIC

Daniel — In His Prime at More Than 90 Years of Age

SCRIPTURES

1. **Daniel 1:1, 3-21** — In the third year of the reign of Jehoiakim king
   of Judah came Nebuchadnezzar king of Babylon unto Jerusalem,

and besieged it. And the king spake unto Ashpenaz the master of his eunuchs, that he should bring certain of the children of Israel, and of the king's seed, and of the princes; Children in whom was no blemish, but well favoured, and skilful in all wisdom, and cunning in knowledge, and understanding science, and such as had ability in them to stand in the king's palace, and whom they might teach the learning and the tongue of the Chaldeans. And the king appointed them a daily provision of the king's meat, and of the wine which he drank: so nourishing them three years, that at the end thereof they might stand before the king. Now among these were of the children of Judah, Daniel, Hananiah, Mishael, and Azariah: Unto whom the prince of the eunuchs gave names: for he gave unto Daniel the name of Belteshazzar; and to Hananiah, of Shadrach; and to Mishael, of Meshach; and to Azariah, of Abednego. But Daniel purposed in his heart that he would not defile himself with the portion of the king's meat, nor with the wine which he drank: therefore he requested of the prince of the eunuchs that he might not defile himself. Now God had brought Daniel into favour and tender love with the prince of the eunuchs. And the prince of the eunuchs said unto Daniel, I fear my lord the king, who hath appointed your meat and your drink: for why should he see your faces worse liking than the children which are of your sort? then shall ye make me endanger my head to the king. Then said Daniel to Melzar, whom the prince of the eunuchs had set over Daniel, Hananiah, Mishael, and Azariah, Prove thy servants, I beseech thee, ten days; and let them give us pulse to eat, and water to drink. Then let our countenances be looked upon before thee, and the countenance of the children that eat of the portion of the king's meat: and as thou seest, deal with thy servants. So he consented to them in this matter, and proved them ten days. And at the end of ten days their countenances appeared fairer and fatter in flesh than all the children which did eat the portion of the king's meat. Thus Melzar took away the portion of their meat, and the wine that they should drink; and gave them pulse. As for these four children, God gave them knowledge and skill in all learning and wisdom: and Daniel had understanding in all visions and dreams. Now at the end of the days that the king had said he should bring them in, then the prince of the eunuchs brought them in before Nebuchadnezzar. And the king communed with them; and among them all was found none like Daniel, Hananiah, Mishael, and Azariah: therefore stood they before the king. And in all matters of wisdom and understanding, that the king enquired of them, he found them ten times better than all the magicians and astrologers that were in all his realm. And Daniel continued even unto the first year of king Cyrus.

2. **Daniel 2:48** — Then the king made Daniel a great man, and gave him many great gifts, and made him ruler over the whole province of Babylon, and chief of the governors over all the wise men of Babylon.

3. **Daniel 5:1, 4-9** — Belshazzar the king made a great feast to a thousand of his lords, and drank wine before the thousand. They drank wine, and praised the gods of gold, and of silver, of brass, of iron, of wood, and of stone. In the same hour came forth fingers of a man's hand, and wrote over against the candlestick upon the plaister of the wall of the king's palace: and the king saw the part of the hand that wrote. Then the king's countenance was changed, and his thoughts troubled him, so that the joints of his loins were loosed, and his knees smote one against another. The king cried aloud to bring in the astrologers, the Chaldeans, and the soothsayers. And the king spake, and said to the wise men of Babylon, Whosoever shall read this writing, and shew me the interpretation thereof, shall be clothed with scarlet, and have a chain of gold about his neck, and shall be the third ruler in the kingdom. Then came in all the king's wise men: but they could not read the writing, nor make known to the king the interpretation thereof. Then was king Belshazzar greatly troubled, and his countenance was changed in him, and his lords were astonied.

4. **Daniel 5:11,12** — There is a man in thy kingdom, in whom is the spirit of the holy gods; and in the days of thy father light and understanding and wisdom, like the wisdom of the gods, was found in him; whom the king Nebuchadnezzar thy father, the king, I say, thy father, made master of the magicians, astrologers, Chaldeans, and soothsayers; Forasmuch as an excellent spirit, and knowledge, and understanding, interpreting of dreams, and shewing of hard sentences, and dissolving of doubts, were found in the same Daniel, whom the king named Belteshazzar: now let Daniel be called, and he will shew the interpretation.

5. **Daniel 5:23-31** — But hast lifted up thyself against the Lord of heaven; and they have brought the vessels of his house before thee, and thou, and thy lords, thy wives, and thy concubines, have drunk wine in them; and thou hast praised the gods of silver, and gold, of brass, iron, wood, and stone, which see not, nor hear, nor know: and

the God in whose hand thy breath is, and whose are all thy ways, hast thou not glorified: Then was the part of the hand sent from him; and this writing was written. And this is the writing that was written, Mene, Mene, Tekel, Upharsin. This is the interpretation of the thing: Mene; God hath numbered thy kingdom, and finished it. Tekel; Thou art weighed in the balances, and art found wanting. Peres; Thy kingdom is divided, and given to the Medes and Persians. Then commanded Belshazzar, and they clothed Daniel with scarlet, and put a chain of gold about his neck, and made a proclamation concerning him, that he should be the third ruler in the kingdom. In that night was Belshazzar the king of the Chaldeans slain. And Darius the Median took the kingdom....

6. **Daniel 6:28** — So this Daniel prospered in the reign of Darius....

7. **Daniel 6:7-26** — All the presidents of the kingdom, the governors, and the princes, the counsellors, and the captains, have consulted together to establish a royal statute, and to make a firm decree, that whosoever shall ask a petition of any God or man for thirty days, save of thee, O king, he shall be cast into the den of lions. Now, O king, establish the decree, and sign the writing, that it be not changed, according to the law of the Medes and Persians, which altereth not. Wherefore king Darius signed the writing and the decree. Now when Daniel knew that the writing was signed, he went into his house; and his windows being open in his chamber toward Jerusalem, he kneeled upon his knees three times a day, and prayed, and gave thanks before his God, as he did aforetime. Then these men assembled, and found Daniel praying and making supplication before his God. Then they came near, and spake before the king concerning the king's decree; Hast thou not signed a decree, that every man that shall ask a petition of any God or man within thirty days, save of thee, O king, shall be cast into the den of lions? The king answered and said, The thing is true, according to the law of the Medes and Persians, which altereth not. Then answered they and said before the king, That Daniel, which is of the children of the captivity of Judah, regardeth not thee, O king, nor the decree that thou hast signed, but maketh his petition three times a day. Then the king, when he heard these words, was sore displeased with himself, and set his heart on Daniel to deliver him: and he laboured till the going down of the sun to deliver him. Then these men assembled unto the king, and said unto the king, Know, O king, that the law of the Medes and Persians is, That no decree nor

statute which the king establisheth may be changed. Then the king commanded, and they brought Daniel, and cast him into the den of lions. Now the king spake and said unto Daniel, Thy God whom thou servest continually, he will deliver thee. And a stone was brought, and laid upon the mouth of the den; and the king sealed it with his own signet, and with the signet of his lords; that the purpose might not be changed concerning Daniel. Then the king went to his palace, and passed the night fasting: neither were instruments of musick brought before him: and his sleep went from him. Then the king arose very early in the morning, and went in haste unto the den of lions. And when he came to the den, he cried with a lamentable voice unto Daniel: and the king spake and said to Daniel, O Daniel, servant of the living God, is thy God, whom thou servest continually, able to deliver thee from the lions? Then said Daniel unto the king, O king, live for ever. My God hath sent his angel, and hath shut the lions' mouths, that they have not hurt me: forasmuch as before him innocency was found in me; and also before thee, O king, have I done no hurt. Then was the king exceedingly glad for him, and commanded that they should take Daniel up out of the den. So Daniel was taken up out of the den, and no manner of hurt was found upon him, because he believed in his God. And the king commanded, and they brought those men which had accused Daniel, and they cast them into the den of lions, them, their children, and their wives; and the lions had the mastery of them, and brake all their bones in pieces or ever they came at the bottom of the den. Then king Darius wrote unto all people, nations, and languages, that dwell in all the earth; Peace be multiplied unto you. I make a decree, That in every dominion of my kingdom men tremble and fear before the God of Daniel: for he is the living God, and stedfast for ever, and his kingdom that which shall not be destroyed, and his dominion shall be even unto the end.

8. **Daniel 6:28** — So this Daniel prospered in the reign of Darius, and in the reign of Cyrus the Persian.

9. **Ezra 6:3-5** — In the first year of Cyrus the king the same Cyrus the king made a decree concerning the house of God at Jerusalem, Let the house be builded, the place where they offered sacrifices, and let the foundations thereof be strongly laid; the height thereof threescore cubits, and the breadth thereof threescore cubits; With three rows of great stones, and a row of new timber: and let the expenses be given out of the king's house: And also let the golden and silver vessels of

the house of God, which Nebuchadnezzar took forth out of the temple which is at Jerusalem, and brought unto Babylon, be restored, and brought again unto the temple which is at Jerusalem, every one to his place, and place them in the house of God.

SYNOPSIS

Throughout our lessons, we have firmly established that it is God's will for us to live a prolonged, satisfied life and to be highly productive in our senior years. If you are young, you may thinking, *This teaching is really not for me*, but that isn't true.

You have parents and possibly grandparents who are older, and they need your encouragement to keep moving forward and believing that they're living in the best years of their life. One of these days, should Jesus delay His coming, you, too, will reach your senior years. And if you're aware of and mentally prepared for living the long, satisfying life that God wants you to have, you will be much more fruitful in your latter years.

Daniel is another prime example of one who thrived all the way into his 90s, and in this lesson we will search the Scriptures to see how God used him to be a beacon of light and an ambassador of righteousness in a foreign land.

The emphasis of this lesson:

Daniel lived an extraordinary life, serving as a royal advisor and high-ranking official to nine different kings over a 70-year span. Because Daniel purposed in his heart to honor God and do what was right, God's favor rested on him, enabling him to interpret dreams and visions and delivering him from a den of lions in his old age.

Welcome to the Greatest Season of Your Life!

Contrary to what most people believe, our latter years are meant to be even better than our early years. Referring to God's people, the psalmist said, "[Growing in grace] they shall still bring forth fruit in old age; they shall be full of sap [of spiritual vitality] and [rich in the] verdure [of trust, love, and contentment]. [They are living memorials] to show that the Lord is upright and faithful to His promises…" (Psalm 92:14,15 *AMPC*).

It is interesting to note that recent studies confirm what God's Word has said all along. Regarding the latter years of our life, the trending statistics show:

- The most productive age is from 60 to 70 years of age.
- The second most productive stage is from 70 to 80 years of age.
- The third most productive stage is from 50 to 60 years of age.

The fact is that by the time you turn 60 years old, you have broadened your base of information and experience so much that you know what to do and what not to do. And by this time, you are better equipped to make decisions faster. Statistics confirm our improvement with age revealing that…

- The average age of Nobel Prize winners is late 60s to early 70s.
- The average age of presidents of prominent companies is 57 to 60 years.
- The average age of pastors of the 100 largest churches in the U.S. is 71 years.
- The average age of individuals who become Popes is 78 years.

Without question, the best years of your life are between the ages of 60 and 80. At age 60, you begin to reach your potential, and this continues into your 80s. If you're between 60 and 70 years of age, you're in the best mental level of your life! And if you are between the ages of 70 and 80, you are in the second-best mental level of your life.

In your first 30 years if life, you *learn*. During your second 30 years, you are *working* and *doing*. And in your third 30 years of life, you *impart* to others what you have learned. This means you ought to plan on living *at least* 90 years.

Daniel Purposed To Honor God

Daniel lived an extraordinary life, spending 70 years of it in captivity in the city of Babylon. During those seven decades, he served as a royal advisor and high-ranking official to nine different kings! History reveals that Daniel was taken captive from Jerusalem to Babylon sometime between the ages of 15 and 17. The Bible says:

> In the third year of the reign of Jehoiakim king of Judah came Nebuchadnezzar king of Babylon unto Jerusalem, and besieged it. And the king spake unto Ashpenaz the master of his eunuchs, that he should bring certain of the children of Israel, and of the king's seed, and of the princes; Children in whom was no blemish, but well favoured, and skilful in all wisdom, and cunning in knowledge, and understanding science, and such as had ability in them to stand in the king's palace, and whom they might teach the learning and the tongue of the Chaldeans. And the king appointed them a daily provision of the king's meat, and of the wine which he drank: so nourishing them three years, that at the end thereof they might stand before the king. Now among these were of the children of Judah, Daniel, Hananiah, Mishael, and Azariah: Unto whom the prince of the eunuchs gave names: for he gave unto Daniel the name of Belteshazzar; and to Hananiah, of Shadrach; and to Mishael, of Meshach; and to Azariah, of Abednego.
> — Daniel 1:1,3-7

So we see that Daniel and his friends were among the best of the best of Jewish royalty. Once taken to Babylon, they were each given a Babylonian name and educated in the thinking and culture of the Babylonians.

> But Daniel purposed in his heart that he would not defile himself with the portion of the king's meat, nor with the wine which he drank: therefore he requested of the prince of the eunuchs that he might not defile himself. Now God had brought Daniel into favour and tender love with the prince of the eunuchs.
> — Daniel 1:8,9

Wanting to honor the Lord, Daniel asked that he and his friends be exempt from the Babylonian diet, which consisted of foods dedicated to the gods and not considered clean by Jewish standards. God gave Daniel favor with the prince of the eunuchs who granted Daniel's request. When you purpose in your heart to honor God and do right, you too will have His favor. The Scripture goes on to say:

> And the prince of the eunuchs said unto Daniel, I fear my lord the king, who hath appointed your meat and your drink: for why should he see your faces worse liking than the children which are of your sort? then shall ye make me endanger my

> head to the king. Then said Daniel to Melzar, whom the prince of the eunuchs had set over Daniel, Hananiah, Mishael, and Azariah, Prove thy servants, I beseech thee, ten days; and let them give us pulse to eat, and water to drink. Then let our countenances be looked upon before thee, and the countenance of the children that eat of the portion of the king's meat: and as thou seest, deal with thy servants. So he consented to them in this matter, and proved them ten days. And at the end of ten days their countenances appeared fairer and fatter in flesh than all the children which did eat the portion of the king's meat.
> — Daniel 1:10-15

Daniel and his three Hebrew friends honored the Lord with what they ate, and the Lord honored them with superior health that was visible to all. When you do what is right, you attract the blessings of God on your life. The Bible goes on to say:

> Thus Melzar took away the portion of their meat, and the wine that they should drink; and gave them pulse. As for these four children, God gave them knowledge and skill in all learning and wisdom: and Daniel had understanding in all visions and dreams. Now at the end of the days that the king had said he should bring them in, then the prince of the eunuchs brought them in before Nebuchadnezzar. And the king communed with them; and among them all was found none like Daniel, Hananiah, Mishael, and Azariah: therefore stood they before the king. And in all matters of wisdom and understanding, that the king enquired of them, he found them ten times better than all the magicians and astrologers that were in all his realm.
> — Daniel 1:16-20

When you purpose in your heart to do right and honor God, His blessing and favor come on you, and you become stronger physically, mentally, and spiritually. Clearly, the favor of God was on Daniel and his three friends. God gave them superior knowledge, wisdom, and understanding in all areas. In fact, Scripture says these four young Jews were *ten times better* than the best of all the Babylonians.

The Bible then adds, "And Daniel continued even unto the first year of king Cyrus" (Daniel 1:21). According to this passage, Daniel served in an administrative capacity from the time of King Nebuchadnezzar to King Cyrus, which is about 70 years.

Daniel Served Six More Babylonian Kings

In Daniel 2, we find the account of King Nebuchadnezzar's prophetic dream that none of the Babylonian wisemen could interpret. God told Daniel what the king dreamed and gave him its meaning. This won Daniel such favor that Nebuchadnezzar gave him many great gifts and a major promotion. The Bible says:

> **Then the king made Daniel a great man, and gave him many great gifts, and made him ruler over the whole province of Babylon, and chief of the governors over all the wise men of Babylon.**
>
> **— Daniel 2:48**

Daniel went on to serve King Nebuchadnezzar throughout his 43-year reign, but then Nebuchadnezzar died. Although the Bible doesn't mention all the kings between Nebuchadnezzar and Belshazzar, the ancient historian Berosus documented them.[1] Interestingly, each of these Babylonian kings kept Daniel on as a royal advisor. According to historical records, these are the rulers Daniel served under:

- After Nebuchadnezzar died, his son **Evil-Merodach** took the throne. He was the third king of the Neo Babylonian empire and is mentioned in Second Kings 25:27-30 and Jeremiah 52:31-34. Daniel served as his royal adviser and high official.

- Next, Daniel served as a royal adviser and high official to **Neriglissar**, who ruled for three to four years. He is briefly mentioned in Jeremiah 39:3,13.

- After Neriglissar, Daniel served as a royal adviser and high official to **Laborosoarchod**, Neriglissar's son, who ruled for only a few months and seems to have been assassinated by a gang of conspirators.

- Then Daniel served as a royal adviser and high official to **Labashi-Marduk**, who was relatively young when he became king and only ruled a short time.

- **Nabonidus** was next to rule as king of Babylon, and like those before him, Daniel served as his royal adviser and high official, but for less than a year.

- The last of the Babylonian kings that Daniel served as a royal adviser and high official to was **Belshazzar**, the eldest son of Nabonidus and grandson of King Nebuchadnezzar II. At that time, Daniel was in his 60s.[2]

The 'Handwriting on the Wall' Was From God to Belshazzar

The details of King Belshazzar's interaction with Daniel are found in Daniel 5. The Bible says, "Belshazzar the king made a great feast to a thousand of his lords, and drank wine before the thousand" (Daniel 5:1). This party really went sideways when Belshazzar commanded that the gold and silver vessels that had been seized by King Nebuchadnezzar decades earlier be brought to him so that they could be used by all the guests to celebrate the Babylonian gods.

Thus, the king and his princes, his wives, and his concubines used the sacred vessels, which were dedicated to the One true God and had been used in the Temple in Jerusalem. The Scripture says:

> **Belshazzar the king made a great feast to a thousand of his lords, and drank wine before the thousand. They drank wine, and praised the gods of gold, and of silver, of brass, of iron, of wood, and of stone. In the same hour came forth fingers of a man's hand, and wrote over against the candlestick upon the plaister of the wall of the king's palace: and the king saw the part of the hand that wrote. Then the king's countenance was changed, and his thoughts troubled him, so that the joints of his loins were loosed, and his knees smote one against another.**
> **— Daniel 5:4-6**

It is interesting to note that when the Bible says of the king, "the joints of his loins were loosed," it means he defecated, or went to the bathroom, in his pants. And, according to this verse, the mere sight of the handwriting on the wall overwhelmed Belshazzar with such fear that his knees were literally knocking against each other.

> **The king cried aloud to bring in the astrologers, the Chaldeans, and the soothsayers. And the king spake, and said to the wise men of Babylon, Whosoever shall read this writing, and shew me the interpretation thereof, shall be clothed with scarlet, and have a chain of gold about his neck, and shall be the third ruler in the kingdom. Then came in all the king's wise men: but**

**they could not read the writing, nor make known to the king
the interpretation thereof. Then was king Belshazzar greatly
troubled, and his countenance was changed in him, and his
lords were astonied.**

— Daniel 5:7-9

Suddenly, someone among the attendees spoke up and said:

**There is a man in thy kingdom, in whom is the spirit of the holy
gods…. Forasmuch as an excellent spirit, and knowledge, and
understanding, interpreting of dreams, and shewing of hard
sentences, and dissolving of doubts, were found in the same
Daniel, whom the king named Belteshazzar: now let Daniel be
called, and he will shew the interpretation.**

— Daniel 5:11,12

The king called for Daniel to be brought in, and he told Daniel all that
had happened. And just as Nebuchadnezzar's leading astrologers and
magicians could not discern or interpret his dream, the present-day
Babylonian mystics could not decipher the writing on the wall during
Belshazzar's party.

Then Daniel, who was devoted to the Lord and committed to doing what
was right, began to unveil to Belshazzar with great respect yet unapolo-
getic candidness the meaning of the writing and the reason it was sent. He
told the king:

**But hast lifted up thyself against the Lord of heaven; and they
have brought the vessels of his house before thee, and thou,
and thy lords, thy wives, and thy concubines, have drunk wine
in them; and thou hast praised the gods of silver, and gold, of
brass, iron, wood, and stone, which see not, nor hear, nor know:
and the God in whose hand thy breath is, and whose are all thy
ways, hast thou not glorified: Then was the part of the hand
sent from him; and this writing was written. And this is the
writing that was written, Mene, Mene, Tekel, Upharsin. This
is the interpretation of the thing: Mene; God hath numbered
thy kingdom, and finished it. Tekel; Thou art weighed in the
balances, and art found wanting. Peres; Thy kingdom is divided,
and given to the Medes and Persians. Then commanded
Belshazzar, and they clothed Daniel with scarlet, and put
a chain of gold about his neck, and made a proclamation**

concerning him, that he should be the third ruler in the king-dom. In that night was Belshazzar the king of the Chaldeans slain. And Darius the Median took the kingdom....

— Daniel 5:23-31

Again, Daniel was in his 60s when he served in Belshazzar's administration and interpreted the handwriting on the wall. King Darius the Mede took over the kingdom, and Daniel served as a royal advisor to him all the way into his 80s. His life is another proof that our senior years are meant to be our best years. Scripture says, "...Daniel prospered in the reign of Darius... (Daniel 6:28).

God Protected Daniel and Delivered Him From a Den of Lions

It was during the reign of King Darius the Mede that we find the legendary story of Daniel in the lion's den. Because God's favor rested heavily upon Daniel and he was filled with an excellent spirit, Darius set him over all the presidents and princes of the land. Of course, that didn't sit well with these leaders, who grew to despise Daniel and looked for an opportunity to do away with him.

When they could find no fault in Daniel, they came together to weave a scheme that they felt would most certainly do him in. The Bible says:

> **All the presidents of the kingdom, the governors, and the princes, the counsellors, and the captains, have consulted together to establish a royal statute, and to make a firm decree, that whosoever shall ask a petition of any God or man for thirty days, save of thee, O king, he shall be cast into the den of lions. Now, O king, establish the decree, and sign the writing, that it be not changed, according to the law of the Medes and Persians, which altereth not. Wherefore king Darius signed the writing and the decree. Now when Daniel knew that the writing was signed, he went into his house; and his windows being open in his chamber toward Jerusalem, he kneeled upon his knees three times a day, and prayed, and gave thanks before his God, as he did aforetime.**

> **— Daniel 6:7-10**

The fact that Daniel was fully aware of the law against praying, and that he went ahead and prayed to God anyway — with his windows wide open — demonstrates that he was not moved by the fear of man or any ungodly rules they set. He was moved by his deep devotion to God.

What happened next was very upsetting to the king:

> **Then these men assembled, and found Daniel praying and making supplication before his God. Then they came near, and spake before the king concerning the king's decree; Hast thou not signed a decree, that every man that shall ask a petition of any God or man within thirty days, save of thee, O king, shall be cast into the den of lions? The king answered and said, The thing is true, according to the law of the Medes and Persians, which altereth not. Then answered they and said before the king, That Daniel, which is of the children of the captivity of Judah, regardeth not thee, O king, nor the decree that thou hast signed, but maketh his petition three times a day. Then the king, when he heard these words, was sore displeased with himself, and set his heart on Daniel to deliver him: and he laboured till the going down of the sun to deliver him.**
> **— Daniel 6:11-14**

Without question, Darius had a sincere love and appreciation for Daniel. No one else in his kingdom was as valuable as Daniel, which was why Darius looked for a loophole to get him out of the predicament in which Daniel's actions had placed him. The Bible goes on to say:

> **Then these men assembled unto the king, and said unto the king, Know, O king, that the law of the Medes and Persians is, That no decree nor statute which the king establisheth may be changed. Then the king commanded, and they brought Daniel, and cast him into the den of lions. Now the king spake and said unto Daniel, Thy God whom thou servest continually, he will deliver thee. And a stone was brought, and laid upon the mouth of the den; and the king sealed it with his own signet, and with the signet of his lords; that the purpose might not be changed concerning Daniel. Then the king went to his palace, and passed the night fasting: neither were instruments of musick brought before him: and his sleep went from him.**
> **— Daniel 6:15-18**

Bound by his own unchangeable law that he was tricked into signing, Darius' hands were tied and there was nothing he could do except allow the situation to play out. His love for Daniel brought him to a crisis of faith in which he went without food and sleep, desperate for a divine intervention. Scripture says:

> **Then the king arose very early in the morning, and went in haste unto the den of lions. And when he came to the den, he cried with a lamentable voice unto Daniel: and the king spake and said to Daniel, O Daniel, servant of the living God, is thy God, whom thou servest continually, able to deliver thee from the lions? Then said Daniel unto the king, O king, live for ever. My God hath sent his angel, and hath shut the lions' mouths, that they have not hurt me: forasmuch as before him innocency was found in me; and also before thee, O king, have I done no hurt. Then was the king exceeding glad for him, and commanded that they should take Daniel up out of the den. So Daniel was taken up out of the den, and no manner of hurt was found upon him, because he believed in his God.**
>
> **— Daniel 6:19-23**

Keep in mind that Daniel was not a young man when he was cast into and then delivered out of the lions' den. *He was in his 80s!* And because Daniel believed in God, he was protected and preserved. However, it did not go that way for his enemies. The Bible says:

> **And the king commanded, and they brought those men which had accused Daniel, and they cast them into the den of lions, them, their children, and their wives; and the lions had the mastery of them, and brake all their bones in pieces or ever they came at the bottom of the den. Then king Darius wrote unto all people, nations, and languages, that dwell in all the earth; Peace be multiplied unto you. I make a decree, That in every dominion of my kingdom men tremble and fear before the God of Daniel: for he is the living God, and stedfast for ever, and his kingdom that which shall not be destroyed, and his dominion shall be even unto the end.**
>
> **— Daniel 6:24-26**

Darius gave God glory and praise for protecting and delivery his friend Daniel, a mighty man of integrity. The king was so impacted by God's demonstration of saving grace that he commanded everyone everywhere — by decree — to honor and respect the God of Daniel because He is the Living God.

This chapter wraps up with the words: "So this Daniel prospered in the reign of Darius, and in the reign of Cyrus the Persian" (Damel 6:28). After serving Darius, Daniel went on to serve King Cyrus the Great, and it is believed Daniel lived until he was nearly 100 years old. He was not an old, broken, sick man — but a man of strength and fruitfulness until he departed.

STUDY QUESTIONS

Study to shew thyself approved unto God, a workman that needeth not to be ashamed, rightly dividing the word of truth.
— 2 Timothy 2:15

1. Read Second Corinthians 6:14-18. It seems Daniel understood the principles lined out in this passage. Upon Daniel's arrival in Babylon, he purposed in his heart to honor God — even in his eating. Although it cut against the grain of what everyone else was doing, Daniel spoke up and asked for a dietary exemption for him and his friends (*see* Daniel 1:8-16). How did God bless Daniel and his comrades in return? (*See* Daniel 1:15-20). What does this say to you about honoring God and not defiling yourself with the things of this world?

2. When the Babylonian leaders were moved by jealousy and pride and plotted together to do away with Daniel, God had Daniel's back! What happened to the people who had Daniel thrown into the lion's den? (*See* Daniel 6:24.) What recurring principle found in Psalm 7:15 and 16; Psalm 37:14 and 15; Esther 7:9 and 10; and Esther 9:24 and 25 does this demonstrate?

PRACTICAL APPLICATION

But be ye doers of the word, and not hearers only, deceiving your own selves.
— James 1:22

1. Daniel was not moved by the fear of man but by a reverential devotion to God. How about you? Do you sometimes struggle with trying to please people, afraid of what they might think or do if you don't do

what they say? Read what Jesus said about the fear of man and write what the Holy Spirit shows you about the following passages:

- Matthew 10:26-33
- Luke 12:4-9
- Proverbs 29:25
- Isaiah 8:11-14
- Psalm 56:9-11
- Psalm 118:5-9

2. With an estimated lifespan of nearly 100 years, Daniel lived a very full and active life. What new insights did you gain about him from this lesson? How do these facts enlarge your understanding of who Daniel is?

3. Overall, what are your greatest takeaways from Daniel's life? What do his actions, his thinking, and God's involvement in his life speak to you personally? What can you learn from him and apply in your own life to bring God glory and honor in the midst of a wicked and perverse generation?

---

[1] Some information on the kings that served between Nebuchadnezzar and Belshazzar was adopted from "The Writing on the Wall," Blue Letter Bible (https://www.blueletterbible.org/comm/guzik_david/study-guide/daniel/daniel-5 .cfm; accessed 12/11/24).

[2] Ibid.

TOPIC

Anna the Prophetess — Spiritually Vital in Old Age

SCRIPTURES

1. **Psalm 91:16** — With long life will I satisfy him, and shew him my salvation.

2. **Luke 2:36-38** — And there was one Anna, a prophetess, the daughter of Phanuel, of the tribe of Aser: she was of a great age, and had lived with an husband seven years from her virginity; and she was a widow of about fourscore and four years, which departed not from the temple, but served God with fastings and prayers night and day. And she coming in that instant gave thanks likewise unto the Lord, and spake of him to all them that looked for redemption in Jerusalem.

SYNOPSIS

So far in this series, we have examined the lives of seven people who experienced great productivity in their senior years. We saw that…

- *Enoch* was 365 years old when he had the most powerful experience with God in his life.

- *Noah* began his greatest season when he was 500 years of age.

- *Abraham* had a life-transforming encounter with God at age 75.

- *Sarah* was 90 years old when God told her she was going to supernaturally conceive and have a son.

- *Moses* encountered God in a burning bush and was launched into his life's calling at age 80.

- *Caleb* was just as strong at age 85 as he was at age 40. And at 85, he asked for a new assignment.

- *Daniel* served nine kings in nine administrations and lived until he was nearly 100 years old, still sharp all the way to the end.

In this lesson, we will turn our attention to Anna, a New Testament prophetess who flourished in her senior years at the time of Christ's birth.

The emphasis of this lesson:

Anna was a recognized, elderly prophetess of God in the city of Jerusalem. She was devoted to a lifestyle of prayer and fasting and longed to witness the appearance of the Messiah as she had been promised she would see. Rather than surrender to age, she was determined to see the fulfillment of everything God had promised her — *and she did!*

The Promise of Longevity
Is Straight From the Mouth of God

We have a promise of long life directly from God Himself. In Psalm 91:16, our anchor verse, He declares, "With long life will I satisfy him, and shew him my salvation." The word "salvation" in Hebrew describes a complete package of blessings, including *healing, wholeness, prosperity*, and *soundness of mind*, which means you don't have to have memory loss or dementia. God wants to demonstrate the fullness of His salvation all the way to the end of your life.

In the beginning of Psalm 91:16, God promises to give you *long life*, and the word "long" is from a Hebrew term that speaks of *length of days* or *longevity*. Furthermore, the word "life" in Hebrew is the word for *days*. So "long life" signifies *long days* or *a very long life*. And the word "satisfy" in Hebrew means *to have enough, to have plenty of*, or *to be fully satisfied*.

To whom does God make this promise? According to Psalm 91:1, long life and the fullness of God's salvation are promised to anyone who "dwelleth in the secret place of the most High" and abides "under the shadow of the Almighty." Therefore, if you are living in relationship with the Lord, you are in His shadow, and you can lay claim to the promise of Psalm 91:16. Friend, God wants you to be a trophy of His grace all the way to the end of your life!

Your Fullest Potential
Is To Be Experienced in Your Golden Years

As we have seen in our previous lessons, the latest statistics regarding the senior years of our life are very encouraging. New studies reveal that...

- The most productive age is from 60 to 70 years.
- The second most productive stage is from 70 to 80 years of age.
- The third most productive stage is from 50 to 60 years of age.

Of course, many people between the ages of 50 and 60 are thinking about and planning for retirement, but they really should be thinking about how to utilize the most productive season of their life, which is right in front of them.

These studies go on to tell us that...

- The average age of Nobel Prize winners is late 60s to early 70s.
- The average age of presidents of top companies is 57 to 60 years.
- The average age of pastors of the 100 largest churches in the U.S. is 71 years.
- The average age of individuals who become Popes is 78 years.

No doubt, the best years of your life are between the ages of 60 and 80. At 60, you begin to reach your potential, and this continues into your 80s. If you're between the ages of 60 and 70, you're at the best mental level of your life. And if you are between the ages of 70 and 80, you are at the second-best mental level of your life.

In our first 30 years of life, we are *learning*. In our second 30 years, we are *working* and *doing*. And in our third 30 years, we should be investing time *imparting to* and *helping* others who are younger.

Thank God for Praying Grandmothers!

Rick shared how when he was a child, he had *seven* living grandmothers! There was his great-grandmother Miller who was a faith healer before the state of Oklahoma was even a state. She traveled around casting out demons and healing the sick.

Then there was Grandmother Cora, Grandmother Jo, Grandmother Renner, Grandmother Faulkner, Grandma Edy, and Grandma Bagley. Amazingly, with one exception, all his grandmothers were mentally sharp all the way to the end of their life, and they lived to be in their late 80s or 90s.

Of all Rick's grandmothers, he shared a special bond with his Grandma Renner. He said:

> Grandma Renner was most precious to me. She lived just a little way from us when we were growing up, and when I was a child, I loved to walk over to see Grandma and Grandpa Renner. I talk about them in my book, *Unlikely*.

> Grandpa Renner was good with his hands, and he made all kinds of things. Grandma Renner was a seamstress and a wonderful cook. She used to make the most amazing biscuits and gravy — I can still almost taste them in my mouth!

Sadly, when Grandma Renner got older, she became immobilized. Although she was brilliant and her mind remained sharp, she lost the ability to get around. Little by little, as she chose to sit still, she lost her mobility.

I remember one day, when she was in her late 90s, I went to see her, and I said, 'Grandma, you're such a blessing!'

'Aw, Ricky,' she responded, 'I'm of no value to anyone.'

I said, 'Grandma, why would you say that?'

'Because I can't really do anything,' she replied, 'All I do is sit in this chair and pray for you. That's it.'

'But Grandma,' I said, 'That's probably the most valuable thing you've ever done with your life. As you sit in your chair praying for me, you have a part in everything God is doing through our ministry.'

For Rick, the prayers of his Grandma Renner really made a difference in his life. In fact, she has always reminded him of Anna the prophetess. As we will see in a few moments, the Lord used Anna to pray for Jesus and His parents at the time of His birth.

The fact is, when you get older, you're really primed and prepared to pray for people more effectively than ever because you have an increased knowledge of God's Word and priceless experiences from which to draw.

Anna Was Well Known in Jerusalem

Anna is only mentioned in Luke's gospel, and she appears in Chapter 2, where Luke wrote, "And there was one Anna, a prophetess, the daughter of Phanuel, of the tribe of Aser: she was of a great age, and had lived with an husband seven years from her virginity" (Luke 2:36).

From this verse, we see Anna was a *prophetess*, which means God spoke to her, and she spoke to people on His behalf. She told the people about things that were going to happen before they happened. Thus, she was a mouthpiece for the Spirit of God to make His will known. And she must have been speaking prophetically for a while because the Bible says she was "of great age."

Something else to note from this passage is that Anna was well known in the city of Jerusalem. This is confirmed by the fact that Luke included many details about her life: her father was Phanuel of the tribe of Asher; she was of a great age, and she had only been married for seven years.

Luke then adds, "And she was a widow of about fourscore and four years…" (Luke 2:37). Knowing that 20 years is a score, fourscore and four years is 84 years. Although the Greek text doesn't clearly state if Anna was 84 years old or if she had been a widow for 84 years, we do know that she was quite elderly. If she had been a widow for 84 years, she would have been about 100 years old at the time of this event.

Whatever the case, Anna was an older person who was recognized as an indisputable prophetess of God in the city of Jerusalem. She didn't move off the playing field just because she was elderly. On the contrary, she stayed in the game and was recognized as a very accurate prophetess of God, which makes sense because she had been walking with God for decades. Consequently, she became very familiar with His voice and could accurately discern what He was saying.

Likewise, the longer you walk with God, the keener your spirit's ear becomes to hear what God is telling you.

Anna Was Devoted to the Lord and Maintained a Strong Prayer Life

The Bible goes on to say that Anna, "…departed not from the temple, but served God with fastings and prayers night and day" (Luke 2:37). The fact that she "departed not from the temple" means she was so devoted to the Temple, to worshiping God, and to the prophetic word He had given her about the coming of the Messiah that she refused to leave the Temple's premises. It also implies that she had living quarters somewhere on the Temple premises.

The words "night and day" are used to describe a non-stop life of prayer and intercession. As a prophetess who knew the voice of the Holy Spirit, Anna kept her spiritual "sails" hoisted to catch the movement of the Spirit whenever He wanted to move upon her to speak.

For years, she had prophetically heard and proclaimed that the coming of the Messiah was near, and she was waiting to see Him with her own eyes.

Prophetically, she forecasted the Messiah would soon appear and bring redemption.

The words "departed not" demonstrate Anna's devotion to be near where the Messiah would one day be manifested. The original text indicates *she did not step away from the Temple grounds.* She was waiting for the moment when the Holy Spirit would move upon her and speak to her to let her know the Messiah was on the Temple grounds.

Think of it... Anna was so expectant to see the Messiah that she didn't take one step away from the Temple grounds lest she miss that long-awaited moment. At age 84 — possibly close to 100 — she kept her faith engaged, and out of deep devotion, she stayed on site at all times for decades as she waited with "fastings and prayers night and day."

Anna's Persistence Paid Off

What else does the Bible say about Anna? Luke 2:38 tells us, "And she coming in that instant gave thanks likewise unto the Lord, and spake of him to all them that looked for redemption in Jerusalem." The phrase "in that instant" means *in that very hour* and is intended to show how synchronized Anna was in the way she was led by the Spirit into the Temple, where Jesus was, at that very moment.

When she entered the Temple that day, she immediately saw Jesus with His parents, Mary and Joseph, and Simeon who was prophesying over Jesus. She was 84 years old — possibly close to 100 — and had been holding on to the promise of God to see the Messiah for decades. Finally, the moment had arrived! After waiting for what seemed like an eternity, she now saw the salvation of God with her own eyes.

When Anna Saw Jesus, God's Prophecy to Her Was Fulfilled

Once Anna saw Jesus, "...[She] gave thanks likewise unto the Lord, and spake of him to all them that looked for redemption in Jerusalem" (Luke 2:38). The word "looked" means *to be filled with a holy expectation to see prophecy fulfilled.* Anna was determined not to be finished with life until she saw the fulfillment of God's promise to her. She embraced the revelation He had given her about the coming Messiah. And when Anna saw Jesus, she immediately perceived He was the One — the Messiah the Spirit of God had told her about. The prophecy had finally come to pass.

With Joseph, Mary, and the Christ Child watching, she prophetically welcomed the Messiah without hesitation or reservation and began to prophesy over Baby Jesus. Indeed, He was the Messiah who would bring redemption to everyone in Jerusalem, Israel, and the entire world.

In spite of her elderly age, she was spiritually vibrant, full of faith, and her faith was engaged. At the age of 84 (possibly close to 100), she lived harmoniously in sync with the Holy Spirit and was led to the Temple premises the *very moment* Jesus was there being dedicated. Thus, she experienced precisely what the Holy Spirit had communicated to her.

There's No Time Like the Present To Seize the Opportunities Before You

Friend, just because you may be a little older doesn't mean God is done with you or it's time for you to park on the couch and do nothing. At the very least, it is time for you to *pray.* If you are chair-bound like Rick's Grandma Renner was, seize the opportunity in front of you and begin to pray for others. This is a moment for you to embrace a life of prayer and pray for anyone and anything the Spirit of God puts on your heart.

Instead of saying, "Well, I'm just too old and I'm not any good to anybody." Begin to say, "These are my senior years, and they're golden opportunities for God to do great things in and through me. I can hear God better now than I've ever heard Him in the past, and I'm going to seize the moments I have to pray night and day for whomever and whatever the Holy Spirit moves on me to pray."

Your senior years are meant to be the golden years of your life. Like Anna, continue to listen for the leading of the Holy Spirit and obey His promptings. The more you do, the more and more synchronized you will become in your movement with Him, and the more you will see His promises fulfilled.

STUDY QUESTIONS

Study to shew thyself approved unto God, a workman that needeth not to be ashamed, rightly dividing the word of truth.
— 2 Timothy 2:15

1. Anna was deeply devoted to God and longed to see come to pass what He had prophesied to her about the coming of the Messiah. How would you rate your level of devotion to God? Are you eagerly awaiting Jesus' return? What does God promise those who are? (*See* Hebrews 9:28; 1 Corinthians 1:7,8; Philippians 3:20,21.)

2. The enemy would want you to believe that God is not speaking or if He is speaking, you can't hear Him. Praise God, neither of those statements are true. God IS still speaking, and you CAN hear His voice! To help you grab hold of this truth, take some time to reflect on these promises in which God declares that you can hear His voice, just as Anna did.

   - **Humility and the fear of the Lord enable you to hear Him** — Psalm 25:8,9,12,14

   - **The Lord promises to instruct you and guide you** — Psalm 32:8; 73:24; Isaiah 30:21

   - **Jesus said you can hear His voice** — John 10:3-5; 14,27

   - **The Holy Spirit is leading and guiding you** — John 14:26 and 16:13-15

   - **The Holy Spirit has given you the mind of Christ** — 1 Corinthians 2:9-16

PRACTICAL APPLICATION

But be ye doers of the word, and not hearers only, deceiving your own selves.
— James 1:22

1. Can you remember your grandmothers or great-grandmothers? Were you close to any of them? Did they influence your life for God? If so, how? Which of your family members has prayed for you on a regular basis, and how have their prayers really made a difference in your life?

2. Over time, Anna cultivated a sensitivity to the voice of the Holy Spirit. Through *practiced listening,* she learned to recognize the Spirit's leading, and she has been living in harmony with Him the day He prompted her to go into the Temple. Like Anna, you can learn to recognize the leading of God's Spirit. Many times, He speaks to us and leads us with strong impressions in our heart. These include thoughts of scriptures, impressions of pictures, and simply the presence or absence of peace to do something. Take a moment and pray, *"Holy Spirit, please help me recognize and hear Your voice. From this day forward, I want to hear what You are saying to me. In Jesus' name, Amen."*

LESSON 10

TOPIC

John the Apostle — New Revelation at More Than 90 Years of Age

SCRIPTURES

1. **Psalm 91:16** — With long life will I satisfy him, and shew him my salvation.

2. **John 21:18-23** — Verily, verily, I say unto thee, When thou wast young, thou girdest thyself, and walkedst whither thou wouldest: but when thou shalt be old, thou shalt stretch forth thy hands, and another shall gird thee, and carry thee whither thou wouldest not. This spake he, signifying by what death he should glorify God. And when he had spoken this, he saith unto him, Follow me. Then Peter, turning about, seeth the disciple whom Jesus loved following; which also leaned on his breast at supper, and said, Lord, which is he that betrayeth thee? Peter seeing him saith to Jesus, Lord, and what shall this man do? Jesus saith unto him, If I will that he tarry till I come, what is that to thee? follow thou me. Then went this saying abroad among the brethren, that that disciple should not die: yet Jesus said not unto him, He shall not die; but, If I will that he tarry till I come, what is that to thee?

3. **Psalm 84:7** — They go from strength to strength....

4. **2 Timothy 4:7** — I have fought a good fight, I have finished my course, I have kept the faith.
5. **Mark 9:23** — …All things are possible to him that believeth.

SYNOPSIS

As we noted in Lesson 1, many people have wrongly believed God only promises us 70 to 80 years of life, and they base it on Psalm 90:10. But that passage was written to the disgruntled children of Israel who rebelled against God in the wilderness and forfeited their privilege to enter the Promised Land. Rather than let this irritable generation wander in misery for decades on end, God mercifully limited their life to no more than 70 to 80 years.

As we've established throughout our study, **it is God's will to bless His people with long life**, and He promises this repeatedly in the Scriptures. The best years of life are our senior years. Enoch, Noah, Abraham, Sarah, Moses, Caleb, Daniel, and Anna were all blessed with longevity and experienced their most productive season in their later years. In this final lesson, we will focus on the apostle John and see how his greatest revelation from God came when he was in his 90s.

The emphasis of this lesson:

The apostle John had a deep revelation of the love of God. Although he was arrested, persecuted, and imprisoned, God gave him an unprecedented revelation of Jesus and empowered him to pen five books of the New Testament — all during his senior years of life.

A Final Look at Our Foundational Verse

Once more, we turn our eyes to God's wonderful promise in Psalm 91:16, which says, "With long life will I satisfy him, and shew him my salvation." God wants to *show* you His salvation, which means He wants to tangibly demonstrate His salvation in your life. The word "salvation" describes a package of blessings that includes *prosperity, preservation, healing, mental soundness*, and every other good and perfect gift He has made available to you through Christ.

Whether you are young or older, it is vital that you understand and embrace this truth. God has no desire to see you become broken down, feeble, or plagued with health issues. He wants you to thrive and experience the fullness of His salvation all the way to the end of your life.

He said, "With *long life* will I satisfy him…" (Psalm 91:16). The word "long" is from a Hebrew term that speaks of *length of days* or *longevity*, and the word "life" in Hebrew is the word for *days*. Coupled together, the words "long life" depict *long days* or *a very long life*. That is what God wants to satisfy you with. The word "satisfy" is from a term that means *to have enough*, *to have plenty of*, or *to be fully satisfied*.

Thus, Psalm 91:16 as a whole is God telling us we can live a very long life until we are satisfied, and this promise is available to anyone who dwells in the shadow of Almighty God (*see* Psalm 91:1). So don't check out of this life too soon. There is an unlimited abundance of God's salvation with which He wants to satisfy you.

Age Makes Us Better, Giving Us Time To Grow

Wine, cheese, beef, balsamic vinegar, fine leather, a cast iron skillet, and your favorite pair of jeans… What do all these things have in common? They are all known to get better with age. Similarly, age makes you better, giving you more time to learn, grow, and gather greater knowledge and experience. Some of the latest studies on aging show that…

- The most productive time in life is from 60 to 70 years of age.
- The second most productive stage is from 70 to 80 years of age.
- The third most productive stage is from 50 to 60 years of age.

These findings are logical because, as you get older, you know a great deal more than you did when you were younger. You have a much better idea of what works and doesn't work as well as what you want and don't want out of life. Therefore, you are better able to discern things and make decisions quicker.

Now if you are between the ages of 50 and 60, you may be thinking about heading for retirement like so many others. While it is certainly wise to save money and plan for the future, you need to also begin thinking about how to make the most of the greatest season of your life, which starts at age 60. Recent studies confirm this, noting that…

- The average age of Nobel Prize winners is late 60s to early 70s.
- The average age of presidents of prominent companies is 57 to 60 years.
- The average age of pastors of the 100 largest churches in the U.S. is 71 years.
- The average age of individuals who become Popes is 78 years.

Friend, the best years of your life are between the ages of 60 and 80. At age 60, you begin to reach your potential, and this continues into your 80s. If you're between the ages of 60 and 70, you're in the best mental stage of your life! And if you are between the ages of 70 and 80, you are in the second-best mental stage of your life.

During your first 30 years, you are *learning*. In the second 30 years, you are *working* and *doing*. And in the third 30 years, you should be spending your time *imparting to and helping* others get a good start. It is a grave mistake for those who are older to think they are irrelevant or have nothing to offer. Clearly, age makes all of us better because it gives us more time to learn, grow, and mature.

The Bible Is Filled with People Who Excelled in Their Senior Years

In these lessons, we have seen that Enoch was 365 years old when he received new revelation from God and was raptured into Heaven. Noah was 500 years old when he was entrusted with the greatest assignment of his life. Abraham was 99 years old when God told him he was going to become a father. And Sarah, his wife, was 90 years old when God told her she was going to become a first-time mother.

We also learned about how Caleb, who was just as strong at 85 as he was at 40, told Joshua, "Give me this mountain! The one that is infested with the Anakim giants. I want one more big assignment in my life" (*see* Joshua 14:12).

Then there was Daniel, who was taken into Babylonian captivity in his teens and lived up to 100 years, serving nine different kings in nine different administrations. As these foreign rulers came and went, Daniel remained the only stable force for more than a 70-year span of time.

Amazingly, he never lost his position even though he got older. In fact, the very end of his life was the most fruitful.

In our last lesson, we examined the life of Anna the prophetess who was at least 84, possibly close to 100, when she reached the apex of her life. God had given her a prophetic word that she would see the Messiah who would redeem Israel and the entire world. For years on end, she engaged her faith, followed the leading of the Holy Spirit, and refused to leave the Temple until she saw the fulfillment of God's promise with her own eyes, which is exactly what she experienced.

The Apostle John
Experienced His Greatest Revelation in His 90s

The apostle John is another example of someone who lived long enough to receive insights and knowledge from the Lord much later in life. If John had died earlier, he would have left the earth before he received his revelation of Christ on the island of Patmos. Hence, he would have missed the greatest fruit-producing season of his life. But because John remained, he experienced his greatest season of usefulness in his 90s and continued to flourish until he died at an old age of possibly 106. Let's look at this "disciple whom Jesus loved" and see what we can learn from what took place in his later years.

Jesus Predicted Peter's Death

After Jesus was raised from the dead and before He returned to the Father in Heaven, Jesus showed Himself to His disciples numerous times for 40 days. One such occasion is recorded in the final chapter in the gospel of John, and here we see John quoting what Jesus prophesied to Peter about what would take place in his latter years. Jesus said:

> **Verily, verily, I say unto thee [Peter], When thou wast young, thou girdest thyself, and walkedst whither thou wouldest: but when thou shalt be old, thou shalt stretch forth thy hands, and another shall gird thee, and carry thee whither thou wouldest not. This spake he, signifying by what death he should glorify God. And when he had spoken this, he saith unto him, Follow me.**
> **— John 21:18,19**

In these two verses, Jesus prophesied to Peter that he was going to die a death he would not prefer, which was, of course, crucifixion. We know from history that Peter was crucified upside down in the city of Rome in AD 64, and he was executed under the reign of Nero. It seems that by that time, many of the other apostles had already been martyred.

Apparently frustrated by Jesus' response, "Peter, turning about, seeth the disciple whom Jesus loved following; which also leaned on his breast at supper, and said, Lord, which is he that betrayeth thee? Peter seeing him saith to Jesus, Lord, and what shall this man do?" (John 21:20,21)

John Was 'The Disciple Whom Jesus Loved'

To understand what is going on in this passage, you need to know that John was referring to himself as "the disciple whom Jesus loved." John gave himself this designation and used it all throughout his gospel because he had a deep revelation of Jesus' love. We know from Church history that John was the youngest of all the disciples. In fact, some scholars speculate that John was between the ages of 14 and 16 when he began to follow Jesus. This would make Jesus twice John's age when they met.

In John's eyes, Jesus was not just his Lord and Master — He was a beloved older brother whom John greatly loved and admired. At the Last Supper, it is recorded that John — the disciple whom Jesus loved — had laid his head on Jesus' chest. This display of affection makes more sense, knowing that John was a teenager enamored by the person of Jesus.

Clearly, John had been greatly impacted by the love of Jesus as a young man, and he never forgot what he experienced. In fact, Jesus' love left such an impression on John that he wrote about that love in his gospel and his three epistles.

The loving relationship between Jesus and John must have been evident to all the disciples, which is probably why Peter asked Jesus, "…Lord, and what shall this man do?" (John 21:21) In other words, Peter was asking, "Hey, Lord, what about John? What's going to happen to him? How's he going to die?"

John, who was an eyewitness to this entire conversation, recorded this rebuttal from Jesus in John 21:22:

> **Jesus saith unto him, If I will that he tarry till I come, what is that to thee? follow thou me.**

Basically, Jesus told Peter, "What happens to John is none of your business. You just follow Me!" Interestingly, the Bible then says in John 21:23, "Then went this saying abroad among the brethren, that that disciple should not die: yet Jesus said not unto him, He shall not die; but, If I will that he tarry till I come, what is that to thee?"

John Was Arrested When He Was 92

History tells us that the apostle John did live a long life and was the apostle who lived the longest. But at the age of 92, John was sent to the island of Patmos as a prisoner of the Emperor Domitian. He began the book of Revelation telling of his whereabouts:

> **I John, who also am your brother, and companion in tribulation, and in the kingdom and patience of Jesus Christ, was in the isle that is called Patmos, for the word of God, and for the testimony of Jesus Christ.**
>
> **— Revelation 1:9**

The island of Patmos was a prison in the middle of the Aegean Sea, which served as a repository of the worst criminals and political offenders of the Roman Empire. Although John was not a criminal, he broke the law by refusing to pay homage to Emperor Domitian and burn incense to his image. Therefore, he was deemed a political offender.

John lived in the city of Ephesus, and it seems that one day as he walked home, he passed by an image of the emperor. By not stopping to burn a pinch of incense to the emperor, John was making the politically offensive statement that Domitian was not god. Apparently, someone noted John's actions of "treasonous disloyalty" and reported him to the authorities. Sometime later, there was a knock at John's door, and standing on the other side were Roman soldiers who had been sent to arrest him.

When Domitian discovered that one of the last living apostles of Jesus was in custody, he was elated. The emperor then demanded that John be brought to the city of Rome and be put on trial before him. At the age of 92, the elderly apostle John stood before Emperor Domitian, who demanded that John reject his faith in Jesus and declare that Domitian was Lord instead. Of course, John refused, and as a result, Domitian ordered that John be boiled in oil.

There were two ways this type of execution was typically carried out. One method involved victims being fried on a huge griddle. The second method, which is the one the Romans most likely used for John, was to bind the victim with ropes, then lower him into a vat of boiling oil a little bit at a time. This was done slowly so the person could experience the full agony of being boiled alive.

The victim's feet would go in first. Then the executioners would lower the person to his knees, then up to the waist. Finally, they would fully submerge him in oil.

Church history documents that after John had been submersed in the boiling oil, the officials gave the order for a flesh hook to be dragged through the oil to pull out his skeleton. When the flesh hook came out of the oil, John was sitting on it, completely preserved by the power of God!

The emperor realized that he could not kill John. Domitian was so terrified at the sight of John alive and well that he ordered John to be exiled to the island of Patmos out in the Aegean Sea. That is the story of how John came to arrive "…in the isle that is called Patmos…" (Revelation 1:9).

Jesus Revealed Himself to John in a Cave on Patmos

The island of Patmos is still accessible to visitors today; it is called the Cave of Revelation. But when John was exiled to the island, it was not nearly as welcoming. In fact, it was a hostile island, and the apostle John, who was elderly by this time, found himself isolated from society and living in a cave.

One day, while living in the isolation of that cave, John was suddenly and unexpectedly caught up into the realm of the Spirit, and he beheld Christ in all His splendor. On that day, Jesus — the One who correctly calls Himself the "King of kings and Lord of lords" (Revelation 19:16) — stepped into that lonely hole in the earth and revealed Himself to John as he had never seen Him before.

John said:

I was in the Spirit on the Lord's day, and heard behind me a great voice, as of a trumpet, saying, I am Alpha and Omega, the first and the last: and, What thou seest, write in a book, and send it unto the seven churches which are in Asia; unto Ephesus, and unto Smyrna, and unto Pergamos, and unto Thyatira,

and unto Sardis, and unto Philadelphia, and unto Laodicea. And I turned to see the voice that spake with me. And being turned, I saw seven golden candlesticks; and in the midst of the seven candlesticks one like unto the Son of man, clothed with a garment down to the foot, and girt about the paps with a golden girdle.

— Revelation 1:10-13

When John was 92 years old, he had an encounter with Christ that was far beyond anything he had ever previously known — a revelation that superseded all his previous experience and knowledge. In that cave on the island at Patmos, John saw Jesus in a way no one else had ever seen Him.

Although John had seen Jesus in the days of his youth and could remember Him well — His face, His voice, and how he leaned on Jesus' chest during the Last Supper — the Jesus who was now standing in front of him was more glorious than he had ever seen. And no one has ever had such a revelation of Jesus. If John had died earlier in life, he may have missed this revelation.

John Penned Five Books
of the New Testament in His 90s

John was so empowered by the Holy Spirit that he outlived Emperor Domitian! When Domitian died and John was released from Patmos, John was in his mid-90s, and he returned to the city of Ephesus to continue his leadership over the churches in Asia. Remarkably, it was after his release from Patmos in the later years of his life that he penned the gospel of John, First John, Second John, and Third John.

Rather than becoming irrelevant and moving off the playing field, John stayed in the game, took a pen in his hand, and recorded all these books — not to mention the book of Revelation, which he wrote while on the isle of Patmos. John stayed active until his death at age 105 or 106.

Rick shared how the Lord spoke to Pastor Kenneth Copeland one day and told him, "I gave My body for you. Now I'm asking you to give your body for Me." Some hear a few Bible messages on faith and healing, and they begin to presume they can eat whatever they want and drive themselves with very little downtime to provide the selfcare they need for their physical well-being.

Oh, how we must understand that there are anointings, insights, and revelations we are only capable of receiving at a more mature age. Indeed, with every new decade of life comes new experiences, new revelations, and new anointings. We must be determined to live long enough to receive the insight, the revelation, and the anointing that is reserved for our senior years.

Friend, there are great things God has waiting for you in the days and years ahead, so don't grow weary and die prematurely. Aim to stay spiritually vibrant, physically fit, engaged in God-given relationships, and on track with God's Word and His Spirit. All of these are vital for longevity. Never forget that you are the steward of your own life — the steward of your time, money, efforts, and energy.

Press into God and press forward into all that He has for you. The best is yet to come. The golden years are not behind you — they are right in front of you! Embrace them by faith and allow the Lord to take you from "strength to strength" (Psalm 84:7). Remember, with God, "...All things are possible to him that believeth" (Mark 9:23).

STUDY QUESTIONS

Study to shew thyself approved unto God, a workman that needeth not to be ashamed, rightly dividing the word of truth.
— 2 Timothy 2:15

1. The apostle John lived an extraordinary life that was not without challenges. What new details and historical facts did you learn about him from this lesson? How does this help you better appreciate the longest-living apostle and see him from a fresh perspective?

2. Second Corinthians 10:12 (*AMPC*) says, "...When they measure themselves with themselves and compare themselves with one another, they are without understanding *and* behave unwisely." When Peter learned from Jesus what would happen to him in the future, he immediately began to compare his life with that of the apostle John, who was a strong rival for him. With whom do you tend to compare yourself and your circumstances? What is it that causes you to do this? Pray and ask the Holy Spirit to show you what's in your heart. Likewise, ask Him to help you avoid the unwise trap of comparison and to help you focus on building a unique, intimate experience with Him.

3. Prior to this series, what was your perspective of your senior years? How is this series helping you rethink your usefulness and the productivity of the later years of your life? Rather than move off the playing field, begin to declare out loud, "My life has purpose! My latter years will be the greatest, most productive years of my life! God has expanded — and continues to expand — my knowledge and experience and has given me a greater anointing and revelation of truth. These final years will be my finest years, in Jesus' name!"

PRACTICAL APPLICATION

**But be ye doers of the word, and not hearers only,
deceiving your own selves.
—James 1:22**

1. One of the greatest aspects of John's life is that he had a deep, personal revelation of Jesus' love. What is your understanding of God's love for you personally? When you look at your life, how do you know He loves you? How has His love tangibly impacted your life?

2. To help you continue growing in your understanding and appreciation of God's love, pray aloud this personalized declaration, which is taken directly from Ephesians 3:17-19 (*AMPC*):

Father, may Christ through my faith [actually] dwell (settle down, abide, make His permanent home) in my heart! May I be rooted deep in love and founded securely on love.

May I have the power and be strong to apprehend and grasp with all the saints [God's devoted people, the experience of that love] what is the breadth and length and height and depth [of it].

[May I really come] to know [practically, through experience for myself] the love of Christ, which far surpasses mere knowledge [without experience]; that I may be filled [through all my being] unto all the fullness of God [may have the richest measure of the divine Presence, and become a body wholly filled and flooded with God Himself]!

In Jesus' name, amen!

A Prayer To Receive Salvation

If you've never received Jesus as your Savior and Lord, now is the time for you to experience the new life Jesus wants to give you! To receive God's gift of salvation that can be obtained through Jesus alone, pray this prayer from your heart:

Jesus, I repent of my sin and receive You as my Savior and Lord. Wash away my sin with Your precious blood and make me completely new. I thank You that my sin is removed, and Satan no longer has any right to lay claim on me. Through Your empowering grace, I faithfully promise that I will serve You as my Lord for the rest of my life.

If you just prayed this prayer of salvation, you are born again! You are a brand-new creation in Christ! Would you please let us know of your decision by going to **renner.org/salvation**? We would love to connect with you and pray for you as you begin your new life in Christ.

Scriptures for further study: John 3:16; John 14:6; Acts 4:12; Ephesians 1:7; Hebrews 10:19,20; 1 Peter 1:18,19; Romans 10:9,10; Colossians 1:13; 2 Corinthians 5:17; Romans 6:4; 1 Peter 1:3

Notes

CLAIM YOUR FREE RESOURCE!

As a way of introducing you further to the teaching ministry of Rick Renner, we would like to send you FREE of charge his teaching, "How To Receive a Miraculous Touch From God" on CD or as an MP3 download.

In His earthly ministry, Jesus commonly healed *all* who were sick of *all* their diseases. In this profound message, learn about the manifold dimensions of Christ's wisdom, goodness, power, and love toward all humanity who came to Him in faith with their needs.

☑ **YES, I want to receive Rick Renner's monthly teaching letter!**

Simply scan the QR code to claim this resource or go to: **renner.org/claim-your-free-offer**

Connect

WITH US!

🏠 renner.org

⭕ facebook.com/rickrenner • facebook.com/rennerdenise

▶️ youtube.com/rennerministries • youtube.com/deniserenner

📷 instagram.com/rickrrenner • instagram.com/rennerministries_ instagram.com/rennerdenise

www.ingramcontent.com/pod-product-compliance
Lightning Source LLC
Chambersburg PA
CBHW071606040426
42452CB00008B/1264